Expecting Great Things

Expecting Great Things

William Carey

Linda Finlayson

CF4·K

10 9 8 7 6 5 4 3 2 1

Copyright © 2022 Linda Finlayson
Paperback ISBN: 978-1-5271-0793-9
Ebook ISBN: 978-1-5271-0910-0

Published by Christian Focus Publications,
Geanies House, Fearn, Tain, Ross-shire,
IV20 1TW, Scotland, U.K.
www.christianfocus.com
email: info@christianfocus.com

Cover design by Daniel van Straaten
Cover illustration by Daniel van Straaten
Printed and bound by Nørhaven, Denmark

Contents

For Irene Howat

Storm at Sea
(1793)

William woke up with a start as he felt himself rolling out of the wooden framed bed. As he hit the wooden floor with a thud, it took him a few seconds to remember where he was. Rolling across the floor, he realized he was on a ship and there must be a storm. Before he could manage to get up on his feet, the floor moved again, sending him rolling the other way.

Cries of "William!" and "Father!" could scarcely be heard above the creaking of the ship and the crashing of the waves, even though his wife and children were in the cabin too. They all managed to stay put except for Felix, who with the energy of a seven-year-old had leapt eagerly from his hammock ready to join in the action. William grabbed the door post and pulled himself up.

"Get back in your bed," William commanded his son, who was walking like a seasoned sailor. "It is too dangerous for you to go out." Then turning to his wife, he said, "Dolly, please don't worry. The ship is strong, and you know what a good pilot Captain Christmas is. I'll go and lend a hand where I can and be back soon."

Dolly's protests were drowned out as William opened the cabin door. In washed a huge spray of water and William clung to the door to prevent being knocked off his feet again. Dolly began to scream, and their infant son let out a shriek. Shaking the water out of his hair and eyes, he saw Dr. Thomas guiding Kitty, Dolly's sister, toward the cabin as the ship bucked wildly. Both were drenched by the sheets of rain falling from the sky. Without words, William held the door open for his sister-in-law to enter the cabin, and then together the two men pulled the door shut with the women and children safely inside.

The wind whipped around the men as they tried to stay upright on the quarterdeck. Realizing their danger, they ran across to the ladder that took them down to the main deck. Here they found a frightening scene. The main mast and fore mast were both broken and lying across the deck, while some of the rigging was hanging over the side of the ship.

"The ship is going to sink!" Dr. Thomas exclaimed.

Just then the ship began to rise on the crest of a huge wave. Both men grabbed for something to keep them from being toppled into the sea. Then the ship plummeted so fast that William began to pray, "Thy will be done, O God. If this is the end, then please send someone else to India." As the ship fell, an enormous wave formed over the top of the ship and then came crashing down. Miraculously, the ship stayed afloat, damaged and rolling in the waves, but safely afloat.

After the storm began to subside, the captain advised all passengers to keep to their cabins or below deck, so that his crew could assess the damage. William went to check on his family and Dr. Thomas returned to his quarters in steerage. The storm had caused a great deal of damage and it took eleven days of repair work before they could continue the journey.

William did what he could to help with the repairs, assisting the ship's carpenter as he jury-rigged a new mast from the pieces of the damaged ones. It had to be strong enough to hold the sails, especially in strong wind. Captain Christmas tried to guide his ship, the *Kron Princess Maria*, into a harbor in Madagascar, but the strong winds and current kept the ship from the port. So, the crew worked with all that they had on board to make the ship able to safely finish the voyage.

The delay caused another worry. They were short of drinking water and not being able to pull into land for a fresh supply, the captain worried how his crew and passengers would last until they arrived at Calcutta. Hearing about the concern, William and Dr. Thomas met together to pray for an answer. Within a few days, the rain clouds gathered and replenished the ship's water supply with a steady rain.

Once they were on their way again, William's three sons burst out of their cabin, tired of being cooped up. They resumed their play that the storm had interrupted, being careful to avoid the crew members who thought the boys were in the way. Others were more tolerant and found ways to teach them a few useful tasks. With the boys occupied, William could return to his study of the Bengali language with the aid of Dr. Thomas, who was working on a Bengali translation of Genesis. William did corral his sons for an hour or so every day to do language work too. Even though they were only seven, five and four, he wanted them to be able to speak the language of the country they were going to live in.

Dolly was occupied with six-month-old Jabez, who was turning into a hardy sailor. He seemed to thrive on sea air, and he rarely fussed when the ship rolled with the waves. Both Dolly and her sister Kitty had been very ill for the first part of the voyage, but now they felt almost at home on the ship. As fearful and resentful as Dolly had been at the outset of the journey, she now appeared to look forward to the new adventure. William was greatly relieved at her new attitude, and grateful to Dr. Thomas. As a physician and friend, he had persuaded Dolly to come on the voyage, and he continued to encourage her whenever she appeared to get downhearted.

William and Dr. Thomas also resumed their Sunday worship services in William's cabin. Captain Christmas had kindly given the Carey family the largest cabin. Not many attended the services, only a couple of sailors and two or three passengers who came from different countries and religious backgrounds. Everyone listened, but William was discouraged that none appeared to take the message of salvation to heart.

In his discouragement, William began to question himself about his ability to preach and share the gospel. He paced back and forth on the deck, praying quietly, seeking comfort from God. While he paced, he also began to think that he was too full of pride in his own abilities and had failed to ask God for his strength and wisdom. After confessing his sinful pride, William suddenly reached up and pulled his wig off and threw it into the sea. He had bought the wig a number of years ago when he had suddenly begun to lose his hair. He knew it was mostly pride that had made him buy it, so it seemed fitting that the wig should now be tossed away. For the next few days, he endured much teasing for his almost bald head, but he took it in good humor knowing that it was the right thing to do.

* * *

The rest of the voyage went well until they arrived in the Bay of Bengal. Once there, with their destination practically in sight, the ship fell victim to the strong currents. The wind would fill the sails and push them toward land, and then the currents would tug the ship away again. After days of this back-and-forth motion, the captain was finally able to pilot the ship to the mouth of the Hooghly River. At last, the little missionary band were arriving at their destination, or so they thought.

Captain Christmas gathered William's family and Dr. Thomas together to explain what they must do next. "You know well," he began, "that missionaries are not allowed in Bengal. The British East India Company has made it illegal to even transport you here, so I cannot keep you on board when the authorities come to inspect my ship." The captain, seeing the distress on Dolly and Kitty's faces, hastened on with his speech. "Please ladies, do not be concerned. I have provided a way for you to enter safely. I have a smaller boat that you can use to sail up the river to Calcutta. If you go carefully, there should be no problem. The authorities are only interested in the big ships."

Dr. Thomas also tried to reassure them. "I will be coming with you. I have legal status in India because I used to work for the East India Company. I can come and go without any problem. So, if I am with you and we are stopped for any reason by the authorities, I can be your spokesman. And you do not need to worry about the Indian people. You will find them very friendly and welcoming. There is really nothing to fear."

Kitty and Dolly exchanged glances but did not look reassured.

Dr. Thomas tried again, exuberantly taking the women each by the arm. "Come now, ladies. Let us get to the work of preparing for the next leg of our journey. We have come this far, and we have all done well. God will take care of us." Dr. Thomas first escorted Dolly to the family cabin and then led Kitty away to hers.

The rest of the family followed. The three boys were very excited and peppered their father with questions about how they would all sneak into the city of Calcutta.

William tried to answer them at first, and then firmly told them to be patient and above all obedient. He did not want any of them to fall into the sea.

Dolly was not excited. William could see the fear and anxiety in her face as she gathered up their clothing with angry energy, and then she threw it all down in a heap. William, recognizing the signs, shooed the boys out of the cabin and turned to face his wife.

"I wish I had never agreed to come with you," she began. "I don't understand why you couldn't stay in Leicester and serve God there. The church was going well, and we were all happy there. Why would you think that God wants us to be in danger in this foreign place? Do you not care about your family?"

William sighed and put his arms around her. "Of course, I do," he said quietly, trying to calm and comfort her. "God has called me here and you know he will watch over us. There are so many people who have not heard the gospel. We need to tell them."

Dolly cried into his shoulder for a minute or two before pushing him away and wiping her tears with her sleeve. "I know," she said with a resigned tone. "I'll finish the packing."

William felt badly for his wife, but he also felt excited. He was going to meet a whole new race of people, speak their language and learn their ways. And best of all, he was going to tell them about the good news of Jesus Christ. Having to get into the country in a strange way only added to the excitement. Who would have thought that God would lead a simple shoemaker half way around the world! He would never have imagined it possible when he was a schoolboy.

Shoemaking
(1761-1777)

"Come on, William," one of the village boys called to twelve-year-old William as he came out of the Paulerspury schoolhouse. "Let's try that big oak tree again."

William did not need a second invitation. Tree climbing was one of his favorite activities. The group of boys all came to a stop underneath the oak tree that stood by the churchyard. There was a moment of silence as the boys looked up and up at the enormous tree. Then the race was on. Who could climb the highest? William knew this tree well. He had climbed it many times but had yet to reach the top. Maybe today he could do it. Working with hands and feet he pulled and pushed himself up through the leafy branches until he suddenly missed the branch he was reaching for and lost his balance. He tried to grab a branch on his way down, but it broke and so did the other branches he landed on until he came to a sudden stop on the hard ground.

As William lay stunned, he was aware of his friends standing around him and whispering. Then, he was conscious of his father kneeling beside him feeling his legs and arms.

"William, can you sit up?" his father asked. "I can't feel any broken bones."

Slowly, William moved as his father helped him. He hurt all over. His father scooped him up in his arms, while he addressed the other boys. "Stay away from that tree! This could happen to you too!"

William's mother fussed over him as if he was as young as his baby brother, but William did not have the strength to resist. He soon found himself in bed with a bowl of soup beside him and his mother telling him to stay put.

William slept well, and the next day he thought he was ready to get out of bed in time for school. He still ached all over, but he found he could dress himself if he moved slowly. However, his mother soon found him in the middle of struggling into his shirt and ordered him back to bed. Disappointed, he let her help him undress and crawl back under the blanket.

"No school for you, and you will need to stay in bed for another few days," she informed him, while gently tucking the blanket around him.

Doing a quick count in his head, William smiled. "I won't be able to go to church either." He found church long and boring. Even so, the whole family went every Sunday to the Anglican Church at the top of the hill. His father, the village schoolmaster and parish clerk, had certain duties during the worship service. He led the chants and responses and announced the sermon.

His mother shook her head and kissed the top of his head. "Rest."

The day was long. William did sneak out of bed periodically to review his insect and plant collections. He had to do something to pass the time. He had started his collections by exploring Whittlebury Forest, just outside of the village with his youngest sister Mary. Later in the day, six-year-old Mary poked her head around the door.

"Mama said I could visit you for a few minutes," she said as she approached his bed.

William motioned her to sit up at the end of the bed and leaned back to hear the news of the school from his chatty sister. Then another head appeared at the door.

"Uncle Peter!" both children cried at once.

With a big grin Peter Carey entered the room. He had been a soldier in the English army and had seen action in the British North American colony[1] during the French and Indian War. A tall sturdy man, his face and arms were deeply tanned from his new occupation, gardening.

"I come bearing gifts for the wounded," he announced with a smile. "In this hand I have a beetle I found in the field this morning." Both children looked eagerly at the specimen in the large brown hand. "I thought it would round out your collection." Before

---

1. Now called Canada.

William could reply, Uncle Peter held out his other hand which held a book: *Robinson Crusoe*.

William was thrilled. He loved adventure stories, particularly ones about faraway places. Uncle Peter had kept them all enthralled with his stories of the New World, and this had given William a desire to travel to distant lands. Especially now that he knew he could not work with Uncle Peter as his parents, and he, had planned.

Peter Carey had a successful gardening business and had taught William about flowers and plants and dealing with their pests. William had been eager to join in his uncle's work except for one thing. After being out in the direct sun for long periods, William began to develop a problem with his skin. No herbal treatments helped to stop the painful scaling and itching. Only staying out of the sun seemed to be the answer. Disappointed, William had to give up his plans to be a gardener. But that did not stop his interest and he liked to learn as much as he could from his uncle.

At fourteen, William's schooling came to an end. His father began to look around for another occupation for him, one that would keep him out of the sun. It was finally decided that he would apprentice with a shoemaker in Piddington, a village a few miles away. William was not very excited about the job, but he was obedient and agreed to go. But there was something he had to do first. He still needed to conquer that oak tree. With his sister Mary and brother Tom following him, he headed for the tree. With steady resolve he began his climb, working his way carefully from branch to branch. Finally, he reached the top. Looking way down at his siblings he let out a great shout of joy! They shouted back. Now he was ready to leave his home.

* * *

William arrived in Piddington in the late afternoon. Finding the shoemaker's shop was easy. A sign with a shoe on it was swinging in the breeze outside a large wooden framed house. His knock on the door brought a young man about William's age to open it.

"You must be William. My name is John Warr. Come in, Master Nichols told me to expect you." John was dressed much the same as William in worn breeches and almost white shirt, but also wore a workman's apron.

William entered what looked like the shop with tools on wooden benches by the large front window, a small stove in the center of the room, and a wall lined with what looked like shoes made of wood. The smell of leather hung in the air.

"This, as you can tell, is our workshop. Master Nichols is delivering shoes to a valued client, so I'm on my own right now," John explained. "We will be sharing a room in the attic. Come on, I'll show you the way."

John led William up two flights of stairs to a small, sloped ceiling room with a large bed. There was one small window, a bureau to hold clothing with a washbasin and pitcher on top. William tossed his small bag on the floor, figuring he would unpack what little he had later. Right now, he was eager to see all there was to see in this new place. On their way back down to the workshop, they heard voices on the first floor.

"That's the master's family. You will meet them at dinner time." John explained as he continued down to the street level.

Just then the shop door opened and in came Master Nichols, a short, rather plump man wearing a tan colored waistcoat over a bleached white shirt, and black breeches, white stockings, and black shoes. He nodded to both boys and reached for an apron hanging on a peg.

"So, you've arrived," Master Nichols stated as he pulled on a pair of light brown linen work sleeves over his shirt sleeves. "Just don't stand there. Get your apron on and get to work."

William exchanged glances with John who shrugged and handed William an apron. Together they followed the shoemaker to his bench. Since John had been apprenticed last month, Master Nichols commissioned him to explain each of the tools. John carefully laid out each one, explaining in turn what each was used for. The hammer, awl and knife, William quickly understood. He was puzzled about the dogs until John demonstrated by pinching a scrap of leather with the pincers at the end of the dogs and stretched it a little. Then John reached up to the wall of what looked like wooden shoes all filled in.

"This is called a last," John said, taking one from the shelf. "The first time a customer comes in for a pair of shoes they need to be measured and from the measurements we make their last. Then each time they want another pair we already have their measurements."

"Don't think that green apprentices like you will be making those anytime soon," Master Nichols interrupted. "That is a journeyman's job, which you won't be for some years."

William responded with a mumbled, "Yes sir."

With a curt nod to both, Master Nichols set William to sorting through a large bag of the scraps of leather left over from previous shoes. He wanted them organized according to size and color. John returned to mending some torn leather on an old shoe. The boys worked diligently while their master continued working on a half-finished pair of lady's shoes. Except for the occasional swear word from him, only the sounds of work were heard.

William was greatly relieved when they were ordered to stop their work and wash up at the pump in the back. The evening meal followed almost immediately. Where Master Nichols was abrupt, his wife gave them a friendly greeting. She served up some cold mutton with bread and cheese and small beer and urged them to eat their fill. The three young children sat and stared at the two young men until William winked at the little girl and she hid her face in her apron. The boys then stared down at their food. William shrugged and took another piece of bread.

And so, William's apprenticeship began. He quickly learned the routine. To bed early with an early start in the morning. Work until it was time to break their fast. Work again until dinner time in the mid-afternoon. Work until the light began to fade, cold evening meal and bed. Only Sundays were different. They were all expected to go to the parish church, although William had to sit with the other village apprentices in the balcony. He was not welcome in the Nichols' family pew. John went to the Dissenting Church in the next village, much to Master Nichols's disgust. John just ignored the snide comments his master made at the end of each Sabbath.

One night when both boys were reading in bed before blowing out the candle, William turned to John. "This *Robinson Crusoe* book is great. I have read it twice already and I like it better each time." And then he added, "It is a lot better than that boring Bible you are reading."

John looked up from his Bible and smiled. "*Robinson Crusoe* is an exciting story, but so is the Bible. How can it be boring when it talks about how God made the world? And there are lots of stories about kings and battles and miracles. Then there is the best story of all, about how Jesus came to die and came back to life again, all to offer us salvation."

William sighed and closed his book. John did go on about God quite a bit and William had learned to stop him before he really got started. "I am going to sleep!" he announced. Sliding under the covers, William noisily turned over, away from the light of the candle and the sight of John reading God's Word.

Life Changes
(1778-1784)

"May I borrow this book?" William asked his employer. William had noticed the Greek New Testament the other day, after he had finished his evening meal. He was always curious about languages. He had found Latin easy when he was in school, so he wondered if Greek was similar. William was surprised to see the book on his employer's shelf, considering that he did not seem all that interested in spiritual matters. Master Nichols's language was full of swear words and he was very free with his slaps and shoves when he was not happy with the work his apprentices were doing. He only took his family to church for the sake of his business.

Master Nichols shrugged. "Take it, but do not start reading it when you're supposed to be working! Now get to your bed, the two of you. And do not burn that candle down to the stub. It has to do you another day yet."

Later, as the summer evening light began to fade, William closed the book reluctantly. He did not want to be the one who lit the candle. John Warr looked up from his book, and asked, "Why do you want to read the Bible in a foreign language? It is easier to understand what God is saying in English."

"I'm not looking for what the Bible says," William replied as he slid under the covers. "I just want to learn the language. It looks interesting. Good night."

"You should come to my church tomorrow instead of going with Master Nichols. You would hear better preaching," John urged.

William ignored his friend and made a small snoring noise.

* * *

February 1779 found Master Nichols and his two apprentices in their workshop as usual. William was now allowed to repair shoes, which he was busy doing when Master Nichols threw down his tools on the work bench.

"A day of fasting and prayer!" he exploded. Both William and John were startled. Their master continued, "More like a day without money! Of course, the king does not need the money, but I do. I must give up an entire work day and spend it in church praying about a war in the New World! What do I care about that?"

John ventured a comment. "We are losing the war with the colonists. I think King George is right to ask God for help."

Master Nichols replied by clipping John on the side of the head. "All you want is a day off to go and see your dissenter friends."

John rubbed the side of his head but said nothing. William suddenly became very interested in the shoe in his hand. He knew he would be next if he said anything.

The next day, instead of going to the workshop, the entire household prepared to go to church without breaking their fast.

"Come with me," John urged William one more time as they came down from their attic room.

William, tired of putting up arguments, finally gave in. Besides, he did not really want to go with the Nichols family when their master was in such a bad mood.

They walked the mile to Hackleton, the next village over, where they entered a small meeting house. It was very plain compared to the parish stone church near Piddington, but it had the usual wooden pews. Once they were seated, William looked around to see who else was there. He nodded to the ones he knew from the village and observed the rest as they came into the building. Most were poorly dressed as Dissenters were not considered good people to hire because they did not belong to the Church of England. William himself had felt scorn for Dissenters until he met John Warr. Then the service began.

William had expected to do his best to stay awake, as he did in the parish church, but when Thomas Chater stood up to preach, William's attitude changed. He strained forward to hear, not wanting to miss a word as Mr. Chater clearly explained the gospel. This was the same gospel John Warr had shared with him, but today he realized that God was calling him to repent and believe. William became a Christian.

William's new found faith excited him. He wrote to his parents and his sisters and brother to tell them the news. William's father, committed to the Anglican Church, worried that his son had made a poor decision, but his sisters were very interested and wanted to know more. They began exchanging more letters with their brother.

William also shared the gospel with his employer, but like the times John had tried to witness to their master, William was told to get to work and stop talking. William and John did not give up. From February to September that year, they witnessed to the entire household and slowly God softened Master Nichols's heart and he too became a Christian. Then suddenly, Master Nichols had a stroke and died.

In the following month, Master Thomas Old agreed to take on the shoemaker's business and he hired William and John as journeymen, the next step up from apprentice. Master Old was a godly man and was glad to hear that both the young men were Christians. The workshop became a better place to work, and William felt settled in his new position.

William continued to attend the Hackleton meeting house each Sunday and prayer meetings as his work schedule allowed. He drank in the words of the preacher and studied God's Word with enthusiasm.

His studies in Greek helped him understand the New Testament texts even better. He also had opportunities to meet Christian friends of Master Old who would often visit the household. Rev. Thomas Scott, the Anglican minister in Olney, was a particular help in explaining the Scriptures to William.

As William's growth in Christ continued, he began to have an interest in a certain young woman in the Hackleton church. Dolly was the sister-in-law of Master Old, so that William not only met her at church, but also when she visited her sister's home. Finding Dolly attractive and a committed Christian, William finally asked her to marry him. They were married on June 10, 1781. The following year their first child, Ann, was born.

William was happy in his home and work life. He decided to add studies in Hebrew and Italian to the list of languages he knew. God had given William a special gift of learning languages easily, but Dolly wondered why he bothered.

"Isn't one language enough?" she teased.

William looked up from the book he was reading at the table by the light of a candle. Dolly was holding baby Ann on one arm, while setting down plates on the table with the other. "I enjoy it," he replied with a smile. "I suppose that you were trying to tell me to move my books from the table?"

"That's right. Ann will go to sleep soon, and we can have our evening meal."

"Good," William began gathering up his books. "Then afterwards you can continue your reading lesson."

Dolly sighed. "If I must."

Dolly had never learned to read because there was no school for girls in Hackleton. William thought she should know how so she could read the Bible for herself. After their simple meal of cheese and bread, they settled down to her reading lesson. Afterwards, they prayed together and went to bed.

During that year William was asked to preach occasionally at Earls Barton Baptist Church. The small congregation appreciated his sermons and even clapped for him, which he found a bit disturbing. Along with his language studies, William began to add sermon preparation to his days when he had finished shoemaking. These studies helped him to grow but also started him asking questions on a particular subject: adult baptism.

William had been baptized as an infant in the Anglican Church, but since he had joined the Dissenters, he was being challenged about adult baptism. In an effort to gain more understanding he began to attend some services in the Olney church and at the Baptist Church in Northampton. In those two churches he met ministers who became his friends for life: John Sutcliffe, Andrew Fuller and John Ryland Jr. He listened carefully to their sermons, had many discussions with them, and finally made up his mind that he should be baptized. Dolly was not convinced, but she told him to do what he thought was right. So, he asked John Ryland to baptize him, which he did in the River Nene on October 5, 1783.

All seemed to go well for the Carey family, even though they had very little money. A journeyman's pay was small, and the churches William preached at could not afford to pay him. But their happiness came to a sudden end when both William and baby Ann came down with a severe fever. Dolly did all she could to care for her husband and daughter. She had no money to go to an apothecary, but she did try some herbal remedies that her mother had taught her.

Days later, William's fever finally broke and he fell into a deep sleep. He woke later to find Dolly sitting on the bed crying. When she saw him awake, she threw herself down beside him.

"I am so glad you are well," she managed through sobs.

William was too weak to reach out and hold her. "Yes, God has been merciful," he whispered to her.

"Not entirely. Ann died last night." Dolly burst into fresh tears.

William missed Ann's funeral because he was still too weak to stand for long. He had also lost most of his hair from the fever and he felt very self-conscious. He grieved quietly, praying for strength. Dolly grieved loudly. William tried to comfort her, but it was many days and visits from family before she could stop crying.

To make matters worse, there was another funeral to attend a few weeks later. Master Old died in his sleep one night to the grief of his family and worry of his journeymen, William and John. What would they do for work now?

Preaching the Word
(1785-1792)

"What do you think of it?" William asked Dolly as he modeled his new wig. He had bought it to cover up his balding head.

Dolly looked up from her sewing briefly, shrugged and returned to her work. She was still grieving her daughter's death and took little interest in life around her.

William was trying to encourage her all he could. "I know it's not the best of wigs, but it was all I could afford." He bent down to kiss the top of her head. "You do not want people to think you've married an old bald man, do you?" he teased gently. When there was still no response, he sat down opposite her, and gently took the sewing from her hands. "I have some news, Dolly. And you need to listen. We are moving to Moulton. There is a schoolmaster job for me there, and I can still do some shoemaking in the evenings. I think a change of place will do us both good, as well as giving me another way to earn our bread. Will you help me pack up our things?"

Dolly looked up at him and sighed. "I will do as you ask. Does my family know?"

William assured her that he would tell her father and sisters about the move and that they could visit whenever they liked. With effort, Dolly stood up and started to look around their tiny home. At least there was not much to pack.

The move to Moulton did Dolly good. She became interested in their new house, which was next to the Moulton Baptist Church. It had been a shoemaker's cottage and was already equipped with a built-in sink to soak leather in, and a work bench beside it at one end of the house.

William enjoyed teaching the village boys. Since the school had few supplies and William could not afford to buy any, he made a globe of leftover pieces of leather to teach them geography. He read them the accounts of Captain Cook's voyages around the Pacific Ocean, from south of New Zealand all the way north to Alaska. As he read the stories of the various people groups Cook met, William began to feel great concern. All those people who had never heard the gospel. Someone needed to tell them.

* * *

Gardening became both a passion and a necessity. In order to supplement his meager schoolmaster's wage, William cleared the area at the back of the house and planted vegetables and some flowers, for color he told Dolly. He enjoyed being able to spend time weeding and tying up plants, anticipating the harvest season. Oddly, his allergic reaction to the sun did not trouble him at all.

For his own studies, he still kept up with the languages he had been acquiring. By now he had mastered Latin, Greek, Hebrew, and Italian, and was working on French and Dutch. None of it seemed like hard work. He just enjoyed the musicality of languages. His reputation for language learning came to the attention of a deacon, Thomas Gotch, in the Kettering church, and he spoke to William when he came to deliver some shoes.

"Mr. Gotch, here are your mended shoes." William held out a pair of buckled shoes to the older man seated on a bench in his garden. "I reattached the buckle on this one and secured the heel on the other."

"Thank you, William," the older man replied looking the shoes over. "A neat job. I will get the money for you presently, but first I have something I would like to speak to you about. Please sit beside me."

William, surprised, did as he was told.

"My pastor, Mr. Fuller, tells me that you are working on learning languages. That is a worthy pursuit. So much so, that I want to offer to pay you for it. No, no," he held up his hand when William was about to protest. "I want to do this. Shoemaking is a fine occupation, but I think, along with Mr. Fuller, that you are meant for other things. I think you should give up the shoes and focus on languages. It will help with your sermon preparation too. So, no arguments. I will pay you ten shillings every fortnight."

William could hardly find the words to thank him. The money was sorely needed especially now that Dolly had told him she was expecting a baby. And if William had to choose between languages and shoes, he happily chose the languages.

William kept up his preaching at Earls Barton church every other Sunday. The sermon preparation helped with his spiritual growth. The small congregation appreciated his ministry and paid him whenever they could.

On the Sundays when William did not preach, he and Dolly attended the Moulton Baptist church. They found a very warm welcome there, but the congregation was dwindling and needed encouragement. They began to ask William to preach on those Sundays, which he was happy to do. Soon both churches began asking William if he would become their full-time pastor. William felt honored, but he knew he had no formal training, so he worried about what he should do. He decided to consult the pastor of the Olney church, John Sutcliffe, and Andrew Fuller, pastor of the Kettering Baptist church.

Both Andrew Fuller and John Sutcliffe had become good friends with William, and they recognized that William had a gift for preaching. And since both were experienced pastors, William wanted their advice about what he should do. Mr. Sutcliffe arranged for William to preach in his church with the idea that he would be approved for the ministry by the

Northamptonshire Baptist Association. William agreed, with some concern. He had never preached to a large congregation before, and not one that was so concerned with doctrine, that they often criticized the smallest misspoken word.

As William feared, it did not go well. He was very nervous and the people were not impressed. However, the leadership did suggest that he should study some more and then come back next year. That is what William did. He studied and continued preaching to the small churches in Moulton and Earls Barton, gaining more experience and understanding of God's Word.

In the summer of 1786, William preached again to the Olney congregation and several of the pastors from other churches. This time he was approved, to the great rejoicing of his friends and fellow ministers. Then William made up his mind to accept the call to the Moulton church. He was ordained the following year on August 1st.

William threw himself into the work of a pastor, preaching, teaching, and encouraging those who were eager to hear God's Word, and disciplining those members who lived in open sin. One of his early joys was baptizing Dolly, who had finally decided to join the church. These were happy times for both William and Dolly. William saw the congregation grow in maturity and numbers, and he also saw his own family grow. Felix was born the year William failed his first attempt at preaching to the Baptist Association. Then along came William Jr. three years later, then Peter the following year and Lucy the next. They were also very busy times. The church was not able to pay William enough to support his growing family, so he continued teaching school and making a few shoes on the side.

As William's reputation grew, other churches began to have an interest in calling him. In 1789 the Harvey Lane Baptist Church in Leicester called him and, after five weeks of praying about it, William accepted. At first it seemed to have been a bad idea. Signs of division and disagreements began to bubble up in the congregation and soon William found himself with a church ready to split. Since he was unable to get the different groups to put aside their arguments, William shocked them all by cancelling all their memberships. Then he told them, they would all have to apply for membership again, and agree to sign a covenant of what they believed and how they should behave. Many of the people did reapply and the biggest troublemakers went elsewhere. By 1791 it was a much happier congregation.

Meanwhile, William was meeting regularly with his ministerial friends in the Baptist Association. They met to encourage one another, to pray together for the needs of their churches and preach to each other. One topic that came up over and over in their discussions, mainly led by William himself, was what should they do about all the people in foreign lands who had not heard the gospel? Some said that God was quite able to save whoever he chose to save and it was not up to

Englishmen to go to foreign parts. Others thought it would be a good idea for someone to go, but who? Some pointed to all the people in England who still needed to hear about God's offer of salvation. Shouldn't they be an English pastor's first concern? And so the discussion went back and forth for a few years, until finally William decided to publish a pamphlet, in May 1792, with the long title: *An Enquiry into the Obligations of Christians, to Use Means for the Conversion of the Heathen*. His main argument was that Jesus had told the apostles to go out to all nations to preach the gospel in Matthew 28:19, and that command was still to be obeyed.

Some of the ministers did not agree with William, saying that command was only for the apostles. Others did agree with William, but advised caution and more discussion on the topic. William refused to give up. He decided to preach a sermon to his fellow ministers to urge them to expect great things from God and to attempt great things for God. The Holy Spirit used that sermon to stir the hearts of all who were present. Instead of wanting to wait and talk more, the ministers chose to move forward with forming the Baptist Missionary Society on October 2, 1792.

"Who will go?" and "Where will we get the money?" became the questions on everyone's mind. Each of the minsters agreed to put in some of their own money, but since none of them were well paid, the missionary fund started out very small. However, Andrew Fuller agreed to be the Mission's secretary and fundraiser.

He promised to travel to other churches, telling them about the mission work and asking for donations.

But who would the missionary be? At first William did not think he was qualified, especially when he heard about Dr. John Thomas, who had recently returned from Bengal, where he had been trying to preach the gospel. William suggested to the Mission Society that they write to Dr. Thomas and ask him to come and meet with them. Even if he did not want to go as their missionary, he would be able to tell them about the practical matters of living in Bengal. So, a letter was sent to the doctor with an invitation to meet with the Mission Society on January 9, 1793.

William felt his excitement mounting as he made his way home from the latest meeting of the society. The events were moving much faster than he thought possible and he praised God for all the provisions so far. However, William's elation rapidly faded as he opened the door of his house. Instead of the sounds of his young children playing there was only the soft sound of someone weeping. His three young sons were huddled together on the floor by the fireplace. Felix was holding three-year-old Peter in his lap, with William hiding behind them. Before he could ask them what had happened, Kitty, Dolly's sister, came out from the curtained off bed chamber. Tears were running down her cheeks.

"Go to Dolly," she said softly. "Lucy died this afternoon."

William's shoulders sagged. His little daughter had been fine yesterday but turned restless and feverish in the night. How could she have died so quickly? Going at once to Dolly, he wrapped his arms around her and cried with her.

Off to Bengal
(1793-1794)

"Where is he?" asked Andrew Fuller at the January meeting of the Baptist Mission Society. They were all waiting for Dr. John Thomas to arrive, as he had written and promised. But time was going on, so the men decided to go ahead with the rest of their program, a time of prayer and discussion. Besides wanting to meet the doctor, the members of the society wanted to discuss what the society needed to do to help whoever they sent out to Bengal. And they also thought sending two missionaries and not just one, would be best. But who should they send?

When the meeting was almost finished, the door to the small Kettering church swung open and in hobbled Dr. Thomas.

"My humble apologies, gentlemen," he began without introduction. He continued to talk as he limped up the aisle to where everyone was seated. "I have injured my foot and was unable to get here any sooner. No, no, please don't fuss," he said, as William and Andrew rose to help. "I can manage. Just more slowly than usual. Ah, that's better," he said as he seated his tall frame heavily on one of the pews. Turning sideways, he lifted his leg with the injured foot onto the seat. Then he pushed aside his dark wet hair from his face, revealing a lively expression and warm smile. "There!" he said. "Now I'm ready for your questions."

There was a pause while all those present waited for one of the others to speak first. Then Dr. Thomas himself began to speak. He told them about his experience in Bengal for the last six years: learning the Bengali language, preaching to the people, and searching for ways to help the people in their poverty. Dr. Thomas described the living conditions, the glittering temples that housed the Bengalis' idols and the strict control of the British East India Company.

Once he finished, William and the others present peppered Dr. Thomas with questions, wanting details on how missionaries could live in Bengal and what they would need the Mission Society to do to support them. Dr. Thomas answered them all with enthusiasm, describing a friendly country that cost very little to live in. By the end of the meeting, it was decided that the Society would send both Dr. Thomas and William as their missionaries to Bengal.

William rushed home to tell Dolly and the children the good news. Only Dolly did not think it was good news at all.

"You want me, when I'm expecting a baby in the next few months, to go to a foreign country with three little boys?" As Dolly spoke her voice became higher and louder. "NO! I will not go! And you should not even have agreed to go yourself. How could you do this to me? To your children?" She collapsed into a chair with tears running down her face.

William was immediately sorry that he had not broken the news more gently to his wife, but he could not understand her violent reaction. Going over to her, he put his arms around her and spoke softly. "Dearest, I did not mean to frighten you. I was just so excited. This is a wonderful chance to help those poor people in India. God has called me to do this, and I want you and the boys to be by my side."

Dolly did not answer. She leaned against William and cried.

Later, as the family sat around the table for dinner, Dolly, now calm, informed William that he could go if he wanted to, but she and the children would stay in England. William stared at her. He had not thought that Dolly would refuse to go. He tried to persuade her, as the boys sat watching each parent. But she would not change her mind.

The next Sunday William told his congregation of his plans. They too were upset at his leaving. Most of the congregation felt their need was more important than that of the people in Bengal, and they told him so. William found it very discouraging, but he would not give up his plans. He was sure that God had called him to be a missionary and he could not ignore a command from God. So, he asked Andrew Fuller to come and speak to the congregation, hoping that his presentation of the great missionary work would help them understand. And it did. After the service, many people came up to William wishing him Godspeed, and some even promised to give what they could to the Baptist Mission Society. William praised God for answered prayer.

However, Dolly's mind could not be changed. William tried every way he could think of to persuade Dolly, but the more he said the more stubborn she became. She called the plans crazy and reminded William over and over that his own father thought so too. However, by March Dolly was worn down enough to agree to let Felix, their oldest son, go with William and the Thomas family. Dr. Thomas' wife and daughter were going with him, so she hoped that Mrs. Thomas would help take care of Felix.

William was relieved that Dolly had at least agreed to this. He felt sure that once he and Felix found a comfortable place to live, then Dolly and the rest of the children would come out to join them. Meanwhile, William helped move Dolly and the children back to Hackleton, to her father's home, where her sister Kitty could help with the children and the coming birth.

On April 4th, William and Felix joined the Thomas family aboard the British ship the *Earl of Oxford* and set sail for India. The ship had to stop at the Isle of Man to await an escort of military ships because England and

France were at war again. While they waited, William received a letter from Dolly. She had given birth to a boy, and both were well. Rejoicing, William wrote a letter back full of love for his wife and children. He tried to ignore his feelings of longing to go back and see them, reminding himself of God's call. However, it turned out he did go back after all.

While they continued to wait for the military escort, Dr. Thomas was arrested for a long list of unpaid bills. The authorities had boarded the ship and ordered him to come with them. In shock, William decided that he and Felix should go with him, leaving Mrs. Thomas and daughter to sail on to India without them. And since there was nothing William could do to help John Thomas, he and Felix headed back to Hackleton.

It was a happy reunion. Dolly was pleased to see William and Felix, sure now that they would be staying in England. They all fussed over baby Jabez, who was content to sleep and eat.

A few weeks later, Dr. Thomas arrived, cheerfully explaining that he had cleared all of his debts. He also announced that he had found them passage on a Danish ship the *Kron Princess Marie*. It would be leaving Dover in June. William was overjoyed, but Dolly was not. Once more she refused to consider leaving England with their young family.

William had no energy left to argue with his wife, but Dr. Thomas did. Over the next few days, he talked and prayed with her, encouraging her to come with them. He told about how his own wife enjoyed living in Bengal. There was so much for the children to learn and experience. And did she not want to be a good supportive wife in her husband's work for the Lord? At last Dolly gave in and agreed to go, but only if her sister Kitty would come with her. Kitty hesitated, prayed about it, and then she too agreed to join the adventure.

It was a great rush to get everyone packed up and ready. They traveled by stagecoach to London and then a second stagecoach to Dover. There they were greeted by Captain Christmas and escorted on board his ship. He settled them into his own cabin, taking care to give the women all the comforts the ship could offer. And then they set sail.

* * *

The journey took five months. There were many wonders to see, dolphins, whales, and sea birds, as they sailed around the African continent and through the Indian Ocean. The weather alternated between calm and stormy, much like Dolly's temperament. At first, she regretted her decision to come, complaining and crying. However, Dr. Thomas continued to encourage her, and baby Jabez, who thrived in the sea air, brought her comfort. By the time they had finally arrived at the mouth of the Hooghly River that led the way to Calcutta, she was almost convinced that the decision was a good one. She felt less so when Captain Christmas announced they had to leave his ship and take a smaller boat up the river on their own.

William, on the other hand, was more than ready for this adventure.

Dr. Thomas took command of the small boat since he had come this way before. He spoke the Bengali language well, and greeted people living on the river. In turn they were invited to spend a night in a small village and enjoy the food they offered. William took the opportunity to practice his Bengali, hoping to improve with effort. He could translate it well, but speaking the language was a challenge at first.

When they arrived in Calcutta, they tried to do so without notice. Missionaries were not welcomed by the East India Company, and so the Carey family had no permit to enter the country. William was counting on Dr. Thomas, who could enter the country legally because of his medical qualification and the fact that he had worked for the East India Company some time ago, to be their spokesman.

What a busy place Calcutta was. Full of people, both Indian and British, all dressed colorfully. The Indian women wore flowing saris and the men long gowns of dyed cotton. The British soldiers who patrolled the streets were in their bright red wool uniforms, and the merchants dressed like Englishmen in shirts, jackets, and breeches. English women wore long muslin dresses and carried parasols to protect them from the sun. The smells of spices and fruits were in the air. That made the Carey children anxious to go and see as much as possible, but the adults restrained them. The children would be lost in no time, especially when they did not understand the danger of being noticed.

Dr. Thomas took charge and led the way to the house his wife had rented. Once there, he and William divided out the money they had been given by the Mission Society. William's portion looked rather less than he thought he could manage with, to care for his large family. He had hoped that Dr. Thomas would let them stay with him, but he soon agreed there was not enough room. So, the next day he went to see what he could find.

William returned later that day discouraged. The money would only allow them to rent a shack, hardly a good place to bring his family. He would have to ask Dr. Thomas to give him more of the mission money. Not only did Dr. Thomas refuse, but while William was house searching, some soldiers had come to the door with a list of unpaid bills that Dr. Thomas had left behind last year. Now Dr. Thomas was required to work as a doctor and give all his pay to the soldiers for the debts. The Carey family had to move out now or they might be noticed and told to leave the country.

Dolly and Kitty were not happy about the shack. The boys, on the other hand, hardly noticed. They were busy exploring the street, promising to go no further. William was disappointed in Dr. Thomas, and embarrassed not to provide better for his family. Realizing he must do something, he decided to look for a job. He went to the local market and began to ask about work, but there was nothing to be had. After a few days he heard about some free land in Debhata, forty miles from Calcutta. By now, Felix was ill with dysentery and Dolly had symptoms too.

"There is a house near the piece of land I have been offered. You and Felix will feel better in a better house," William told Dolly. "We will need to take a boat down another river, but it will take us right to the house."

Dolly, realizing it was the best thing to do, gathered up their few belongings while Kitty corralled William Jr. and Peter, and carried baby Jabez. William carried Felix to the boat, and they all sailed down the saltwater river. But when they arrived, the house was already occupied and the people refused to move. Now what would they do?

Mudnabatti
(1794-1797)

"I'm not going with you," Kitty announced. "I'm going to stay here and marry Charles."

Both William and Dolly stared at her, unable to speak at first. They were all sitting in the bungalow belonging to Charles Short, the East India Company's Salt Company assistant. He had felt sorry for the Carey family when they arrived in Debhata to find their promised house occupied. So, he invited them to live with him until William could sort out what to do. Mr. Short had taken a fancy to Kitty and she to him, and they were often found together talking and laughing.

William didn't know what to say. He, along with eight-year-old Felix, had been working hard to clear land across the river from the bungalow to build their own house with a garden to supply them with food. But the area was densely forested, and it was hard, slow work. After four months, he was coming to the conclusion that he wouldn't be able to make a go of it. Meanwhile, Dolly was full of fears for their young boys who loved to run about the forest. She feared a tiger or leopard might attack them or maybe a poisonous snake or crocodile would bite them. So when William received a letter from Dr. Thomas about a job at an indigo factory further north, she and William agreed that they should move. But they had not counted on Kitty staying behind.

Finally finding her voice, Dolly exclaimed, "You can't! I need you to help me. How can I possibly take care of the boys and everything else in this foreign place without you?"

William added in his comments too. "As noble a man as Charles is, he is not a Christian, Kitty. How can you consider marrying a non-Christian?"

Kitty would not be persuaded against her plan to marry, even after Dolly pleaded with her and then grew angry.

With sad hearts and tears, the family began the 250-mile journey north. Travel through Bengal was mainly by river, which meant navigating several rivers over four weeks to finally arrive in Mudnabatti, a small village on the Tangon River.

They were warmly greeted by the village people, who showed them to their new house. Dolly was pleased to now have a home of her own and that it came with a few servants. That would help to make up for the loss of Kitty's help, but not for the companionship.

Once he had settled his family in their new house, William went with some of the workers to view the indigo works and surrounding area. They showed him the fields of the blue flowering indigo plants, the building where the harvested plants were soaked in water and fermented, the place where the mixture was dried on large sheets, and then finally to where they mixed the blue leaves with alkaline and shaped them into small cakes to dry. After the tour, William understood why it took ninety people to run the entire factory.

William also realized that these workers could be his congregation, and he already began to make plans in his head to invite them and the rest of the village to hear the gospel preached on Sundays. However, he had not counted on their insistence on observing their own religion. In fact, before the Hindu workers would begin to work for him, they wanted him to come with them to sacrifice to their goddess, Kali. William was horrified when he saw the idol: a female form with many arms, wearing a long necklace of human heads.

"You cannot worship this horrible thing! It is evil. God is the only true God, not this thing! I will not sacrifice to it and you should not either. Please, we need to leave this place. Come away and learn about the true God."

The workers stood about looking at William and muttered to each other. Finally, they allowed William to lead them away, but they were not happy. They went to their homes rather than listen to William tell them about God's love and mercy.

The next day, William walked by the idol in her special grove and saw that the workers must have come back later, because a small goat lay dead on the ground before it. William was distressed and prayed all the way to the factory that God would change their hearts and bring the people out of the darkness of idolatry and into the light of the Gospel.

Life was no easier for Dolly than it had been in Calcutta or Debhata. She loved her children and tried hard to protect them from the dangers that lurked in the forest, but it was difficult to contain the exuberant boys, now ages eight, six, five and one. She kept Jabez close to her, but the others were more difficult to contain. William did give the three oldest lessons to do while he was away at the factory, but they also wanted to run and play.

Then illness struck the family. The fever started among the factory workers, who passed it on to William, and William passed it on to Peter, their five-year-old. William was very ill for a few days and then seemed to recover, only to relapse for another ten days. When Dr. Thomas heard about William's illness, he came from Malda, where he was now working, to help take care of him. As William was slowly recovering, Peter appeared to follow the same pattern. Dolly nursed him as best she could, but instead of recovering, Peter died.

Dolly was beside herself with anger and grief, and she shouted at William, saying it was all his fault for bringing them to this awful place. William too was full of grief and tried to comfort his wife, but she either raged at him or retreated into silence.

While the villagers were very sorry to hear of Peter's death, none of them would help with a coffin or the burial, not even the Careys' servants. Hindus burned their dead, and they thought they would be polluted if they came near a dead body of another religion. So, William and his oldest son Felix made the coffin themselves and carried it to a place at the edge of their property to bury Peter.

Other things added to their grief. Even though William preached often to his workers and others in the village, telling them about Jesus and his loving sacrifice for their sins, none were converted. They listened patiently to him, but then the Hindus went back to holding their festivals and worshiping their idols. William became very discouraged.

They had not received any letters from England since they had arrived in Bengal. William had written many letters home, to his sisters and father, and to his friends in the Baptist Missionary Society, but there had not yet been any replies. The French Revolutionary Wars raging in Europe meant that British ships, carrying the mail and other supplies, had a difficult time getting safely between Britain and India.

William did continue to work on his translation of books of the Bible into Bengali. He and Dr. Thomas had begun work on Genesis on the ship two years ago, and now William was able to complete it. He was also working on Exodus, Matthew, and Mark, and making good progress. He was pleased that his older sons had picked up the Bengali language and were able to converse easily in the village. Their spiritual life was also a matter of concern for William, so he gathered his family together each night to read the Bible and pray together. He would challenge his sons to take God's Word seriously and hide it in their hearts.

Dolly was not doing well. Her moods alternated between anger and silence. William tried to comfort her, and occasionally she would respond, clinging to him and crying. Other times she ignored him or shouted angry accusations at him, blaming him for all their troubles. William worried constantly about her, praying that God would help her. Every morning, as he walked to the factory, William prayed for his family, one by one, pleading with God to protect and care for them.

Later that year, Dolly announced that she was expecting a child. William was overjoyed. Surely having a new baby to care for and cuddle would help her to get over the grief and anger of Peter's death. And it did help, for a while. Baby Jonathan was a content baby, and Dolly carried him everywhere. But soon the mood swings returned. She directed her anger and her silences only at William. With the children she was over protective, wanting to know where they were every moment, worried something would happen to them. Then one day she began to follow William to work, calling out her angry accusations for all to hear. The Bengali villagers did not know what to do. They were sorry for Dolly, but none would come near her, for fear of her turning on them. William tried to placate her, but it only made her call out all the more. Finally, one day when he returned from the factory, Dolly was waiting for him with a knife in her hand, while the boys were huddled at the far end of the room.

"Get out of here!" she shouted. "You can't come near my children ever again!"

"Dolly, please, put the knife down. I won't hurt you or the children," he pleaded.

But it was no good. Dolly would not listen, so William backed out of the door, frantically praying for wisdom. Then he thought about Dr. Thomas living in Malda, thirty-two miles down the river. He had to get help for his poor wife. He was desperately afraid she was going insane.

Dr. Thomas was only too glad to help his friend. Together they rushed back to the house. They found Dolly sitting in a chair, holding baby Jonathan, and staring off vacantly. The older boys were outside, and William told them to stay there. Dr. Thomas spoke quietly to Dolly, carefully removing the eight-month-old baby from her arms and handing him to William. Slowly, Dolly responded to Dr. Thomas's suggestions that she lie down and he would give her a powder mixed in some water to help her sleep. She allowed him to lead her to the bedroom, and she obediently drank the medicine he prepared for her. Once she fell asleep, he closed the door and joined William who was sitting with the baby.

"Is she alright?" William asked eagerly.

"She is sleeping now," Dr. Thomas replied. "But I fear she is not alright. I think the first thing you should do is get a lock for the bedroom door. If she becomes violent again, it would be wise to lock her in until she calms down. It is the only solution I can see just now."

William set his now restless son on the floor to play, while the older boys drifted back into the house. As kindly as he could, Dr. Thomas explained to them all that Dolly was ill in her mind, and there were no medicines to make her better. All they could do for now was take care of her as best they could. He would come back and check on her every few days.

After Dr. Thomas left and the boys went to bed, William was on his knees praying as he never had before. He prayed for healing for Dolly and for wisdom to know what to do. Should he get someone to come and take care of her? Should he take her back to England and put her in Bedlam, the hospital for the insane? What would happen to the missionary work he was supposed to be doing? Did he get it wrong? Did God not want him to stay in Bengal? What should he do?

Monsoon!
(1798-99)

Dolly did not get better. William hired a servant to care for her, and another to care for his sons, because his job was taking him away from home more often. He was now supervising several indigo farms and he traveled up and down the Tangon River with two boats. One held his bed, table and chair and a lamp, while the other boat held his cooking utensils and supplies. These trips, along with supervising his workers, were also good opportunities to preach in villages along the river. William used every chance he had to share the good news of Jesus Christ.

When he wasn't preaching, William worked diligently to complete his translation of the New Testament books into Bengali. He was eager that the people should be able to read the gospel in their own language. But to do so, William needed to get it printed. When letters finally began to arrive from England, William took the opportunity to write back to the Baptist Mission, asking for money to buy a printing press. He also asked for more missionaries to be sent, and especially one who could operate the printing machine.

William still could not report any Indian converts to the Mission. As polite as the people were, they could see no need to give up their religion. However, William did have the joy of baptizing two new European converts: a young cousin of Dr. Thomas's, and a Portuguese merchant. Both these men helped establish small churches in the areas where they lived.

William was learning a great deal about the way the Bengali society was organized and about their religion. The Indian Hindu society had a caste system that divided the people into categories: Brahmin (teachers and priests), Kshatriya (warriors and nobles), Vaishya (farmers and traders), and Shudra (farm workers and servants). There were also the Dalits or untouchables, who were not allowed to associate with any other caste. William could speak to all these people, but there were complicated rules about how they behaved with each other, especially around eating, marriage and worship. William did his best not to offend the people, but he did not stop preaching the way of salvation to them.

Hindu Brahmin taught the people that their sins could be washed away by dipping in the Ganges River during certain festival times. They also taught that the people must live moral lives, treating all people and animals with kindness. In this way they would be preparing themselves for their 'next life'. They believed that each time an animal or person died, they came back as someone else who was either better or worse than what they had been. It all depended on how many kind or righteous acts they had done. And it was important for all Hindus to attend the temple festivals and sacrifice to their idol gods.

William found it difficult to teach the people that forgiveness of sins only came from God, and only through his Son Jesus who died in their place to take away their sins. They thought they already had a way to deal with sin and their idols would help them. William often found it was easier to talk to people one or two at a time, when he could tell them about God's love and mercy and answer their many questions. The Brahmin, in particular, were eager to discuss new ideas, but in the end, they saw no reason to change their religion. It was very discouraging.

One thing William did learn from the Brahmin priests was that the old language, Sanskrit, was considered a very valuable language. Only the most important ideas were written in Sanskrit. That gave William an idea. He would learn Sanskrit, and then translate the Bible into that language too, to show the Brahmins that the gospel was the most important idea of all.

As William traveled up and down the Tangon River, he began to notice how the people used the land. He became concerned that often very fertile land was just allowed to become overgrown and become sanctuary for wild animals. This was both a danger to the people living in that area and a waste of valuable crop land. William began to make a note of the places that could be used for agriculture. He was also concerned about the forested areas, that they not become entirely cut down. He saw that an overall plan of cultivating both the land and the forests was needed. So, William saved his notes, planning to share them with government officials if he got the opportunity.

* * *

William also saw some terrible Hindu rituals. Unwanted children, especially girls, were left in the forest to die. Or a mother might give her baby to be sacrificed to an idol or thrown in the river to make a god happy. William tried to stop the people from doing this, but they wouldn't listen.

One day, when William was upriver checking in with his workers at one of the indigo fields, he heard some music and chanting.

"What's going on?" he asked one of the workers. "Is it a festival time?"

"No," came the reply. "One of the Brahmin teachers has died. They are going to burn his body and his wife."

At first William thought the worker meant that the wife had died too, so he decided to go to pay his respects to the grieving family. But when he arrived at the clearing, he was horrified at what he saw. The Brahmin man was dead. His body was laid out on a neat pile of wood. Then they led his young wife to the pyre, and she climbed up. She stood for a minute or two while people clapped and chanted, and then she lay down beside her dead husband. Lastly, some of the men covered them over with leaves and bamboo poles and lit the fire. William tried to stop them, shouting and pleading, but the people ignored him as they shouted and danced while the fire burned. When he couldn't watch anymore, he ran back to his boat, full of anger and grief. He made a promise to himself and to God, that he would fight against this evil practice called suttee, until it was stamped out for good.

* * *

In 1799, the monsoon season arrived as usual in June. William expected that there would be lots of rain as in previous years, but this year turned out to be much worse. The rain began and didn't stop. It came in torrents day after day, swelling the rivers until they finally rose so high that the water flooded over the banks. Water ran everywhere, through the factory itself and filling up the fields of indigo plants. And still the water rose so that villages along the river banks were in danger of being washed away.

William stood in his house, which was further back from the Tangon River, watching out the window as the rain came down in sheets and water crept closer and closer to the garden he had so carefully planted in the spring. In the six years he had been in Bengal, he had never seen a monsoon season like this one. He knew he was watching his job being washed away. There would be no saving the indigo plants or the factories after they had been so badly flooded.

* * *

Once the monsoon season passed and the water receded back to the river, a letter arrived from a group of English missionaries that had been sent to Bengal by the Baptist Mission. William was so excited that he went to find Dolly to tell her. Dolly was sitting quietly in her room sewing up some tears in one of the boy's shirts. She looked up briefly and then went back to her sewing. Her servant caregiver nodded to William and then sat quietly in a chair by the window.

"Listen to this, my dear," William said as he sat down on the bed. "We have had a letter saying more missionaries are going to join us. Let's read it together."

Dolly didn't respond. She just kept on sewing. She was having a quiet day, for which William was grateful. He wanted to talk to her, even if she didn't really listen to him. It helped him feel less lonely.

"Oh no," William said a moment later as he read further into the letter. "The British East India Company is refusing to let them into the country. They are stranded on a ship without supplies, and one of the men has already died. This is terrible."

William quickly read the rest of the letter and stood up and began to pace the room. These missionaries needed help as soon as possible, and there was a solution. Colonel Bie, the Governor of a Danish settlement north of Calcutta, had offered them a place to stay in his territory. Should the missionaries go there, and would William join them?

William knew his job at the factory was finished. There was too much damage to rebuild it. And he was lonely here in Mudnabatti with his wife so unwell in her mind. It would be wonderful to have others to join in the mission work he had been sent to do. But would it be right to leave all the people he had been preaching to and teaching over the years? They may yet become Christians. What would God want him to do?

"Dolly, would you like to move away from this place?" William asked her, kneeling down in front of her.

She kept on sewing as if she hadn't heard William's question.

William sighed. Then he went away to write back to the missionaries and to Colonel Bie, accepting his kind invitation.

It took several weeks to pack up all their belongings which had accumulated over the six years they had lived in Mudnabatti. William went around to the villages in the area to say goodbye, and he paid a visit to Peter's grave at the foot of their property. He was sad to leave, but also excited to meet his new colleagues and begin a new work in Serampore, the Danish settlement.

Serampore
(1800-1805)

The Carey family arrived in the Danish territory of Serampore on January 10, 1800. As usual, they had traveled by boat, starting on the Ganges River, then made a westward turn to the Padma River and finally to the Hooghly River that took them to their new home. Even though Serampore was only twelve miles from Calcutta, the missionaries were safe from the British East India Company because this area belonged to Denmark.

Colonel Bei, the Danish governor, welcomed all the missionaries, including William and his family, in his government house.

"Ladies and Gentlemen," he began, with a large smile on his face. "I am so glad that you are all here. While we belong to different denominations, I am a Lutheran and you are Baptists, we both want the same thing: to tell the Bengali people about the one true God. I can use my position as governor to give you all the help and protection I can. First, you need a place to live. There is a large house available nearby that has enough apartments in it to house all your families. The house is yours. Also, I will build you a church, once you tell me exactly what you want. I sincerely hope we can all work together for the good of the Bengali people and the glory of God!"

William was thrilled. He had almost given up the idea of being a full-time missionary, but now God had provided that opportunity. And God had given him more missionaries to work with him. He would not be lonely anymore. William praised God for the great things he was doing.

The Mission House was just what the missionary group needed. There were small and large apartments, which were divided between them all depending on the size of their families. The Carey family, with their four boys, was the largest family. Joshua and Hannah Marshman had two children, John Fountain and his wife had one son. Mrs. Grant, whose husband had died on the ship, was given an apartment for her and her two children. Mr. and Mrs. Brunsdon and William Ward, a single man, each chose smaller flats. They all then decided to use the larger rooms on the main floor as their communal dining room, kitchen, and chapel. In this way they could become one large family, all working together.

William was concerned that all the missionaries should get along with each other, since they were living so close together, so he set up a schedule with the help of Joshua Marshman and William Ward. The entire group would eat their meals together. On Saturday evenings, they would meet to discuss any difficulties or upsets that anyone had experienced that week. William wanted everyone to feel comfortable speaking about anything that bothered them, so that nothing festered and grew into anger or hatred. On Sundays, they met for worship in their chapel and each of the missionaries took turns preaching.

During the week there was much to do. Hannah Marshman became the person who ordered the supplies for the kitchen and supervised the servants who did the cooking. She also became Dolly's main caregiver. Hannah seemed to have the right touch with Dolly and could often quiet her angry moods far more quickly than the others. The other wives also took turns caring for Dolly, so that she never felt abandoned or ignored.

William Ward was a printer, so he set about buying a printing press and setting up a shop to print the Bible translations that Carey was working on, every chance he had. Mr. Ward hired some Bengali men who were interested in learning the printing trade. Then he noticed the Carey boys, particularly the two oldest.

"William," Mr. Ward said, "Your sons are behaving badly, particularly Felix and William. They are wild and disrespectful, and you don't seem to do anything about it."

William sighed. "I know they can be rebellious at times, but what can I do? They no longer have their mother to care for them, and I'm too busy with the mission work."

Mr. Ward shook his head. "I have an idea. Those boys need something to do to keep them out of mischief. Will you let me train them to work in the print shop?"

William agreed. He knew he wasn't being a good father to let his sons run wild, so he was relieved to hear Mr. Ward's plan. The next day, fifteen-year-old Felix and twelve-year-old William were invited to help in the print shop. Over the next few months, Mr. Ward not only taught them the printing trade but also spoke to them about their behavior and their need to repent and turn to God. Mr. Ward was a kind, gentle man, and soon the boys came to love him and want to please him. By the end of the first year in Serampore, both boys' behavior had changed and they professed faith, much to their father's joy.

Joshua and Hannah Marshman had plans to start schools. Hannah was very concerned that Bengali girls never went to school, and she wanted to give them a chance to learn to read and write in their own language. Together, they opened a school for girls and one for boys. Both of them were boarding schools, which meant the students lived in dormitories and their parents paid their fees. This income paid for the running of the schools. Joshua also opened a free day school for children whose families were unable to pay fees. When he wasn't teaching or preaching, Joshua Marshman also helped with translation work.

He was very quick to learn Bengali and some of the other dialects.

William Carey continued his translation work, and was very pleased when William Ward was able to print the first copies of the Gospel of Matthew on the new printing press. He was also busy preaching in the area, and when he wasn't doing either of those things, he was gardening. He dug up a large area near the Mission House and planted vegetables and flowers to help feed and beautify the Mission House. He worked in the garden most mornings, using the time to also meditate on God's Word and pray. Then in the afternoons he went out preaching, and did his translating in the evenings.

With the Mission House fully set up, the men decided that street preaching was the best way to go about spreading the gospel. They joined large groups of Bengalis at their festivals, or set up in the market places and preached God's Word. Many listened politely but then walked away. Some became angry and threw sticks at them. But the missionaries didn't give up. At least two or more of them went out every day preaching or distributing leaflets with the gospel message written in Bengali. Then one day, near the end of the first year in Serampore, something wonderful happened.

* * *

A young Bengali boy came running to the Mission House, calling for William.

"Mr. Carey," he gasped out as he paused to catch his breath. "Come quick! There's been an accident!"

Then, not waiting for a response, the young boy raced away to the Hooghly River. William, Joshua Marshman and Dr. Thomas ran after him. When they arrived, they found Kristna Pal, a devoted Hindu Brahmin, lying on the steps leading down to the river. He was in pain and unable to move, so the missionaries carefully lifted him up and onto the riverbank. Dr. Thomas saw at once that the man's shoulder had been dislocated by the fall.

"I can help you," Dr. Thomas said, "if you will let me."

"Yes, please," Kristna groaned, closing his eyes as a wave of pain came over him.

"William, Joshua, help me lift him over to the tree. Stand him up. That's right. Now we need to find some rope or vines to secure him so he doesn't move," Dr. Thomas instructed.

William ran to the Mission House and found some rope in the gardening shed. Hurrying back, he and Joshua tied the rope around Kristna and the tree. Then with a quick movement, Dr. Thomas grabbed Kristna's arm and snapped it back into his shoulder. Kristna let out a loud cry and then leaned against the tree with a dazed look. The missionaries quickly untied the rope and eased the man to sit on the ground.

"Thank you!" Kristna said. "It doesn't hurt anymore. You have been very kind. I was going to the river to wash away my sins and I slipped on the steps."

"There is no need to go to the river," William replied. "Jesus will forgive your sins just by asking him."

And he quoted 1 John 1:9: "If we confess our sins, he is faithful and just to forgive us our sins and to cleanse us from all unrighteousness."

Kristna was interested. "I just have to ask?"

William nodded and handed him one of the leaflets they had been giving out on the streets. "Here are some more Bible verses for you to read and know that God loves you and wants to forgive all who come to him."

Kristna took the leaflet and promised to read it. The next day, he arrived at the Mission House with lots of questions and wanting to know the truth about God. He explained that he had been trying for years to say enough mantras and do enough good works to please his gods, but he never felt that it was enough. William joyfully welcomed him to a Bible study group they were having. Kristna came every day after that, and brought his wife and daughter too. As the missionaries explained the gospel in detail, Kristna began to understand how Christ's sacrifice on the cross had taken care of his sins, if only he would believe. Kristna Pal became the first Bengali convert to Christianity in Bengal.

The conversion caused quite a stir in the community. As part of his Brahmin caste, Kristna should not be associating with the missionaries, and his friends and relatives became angry with him. And even worse, when Kristna actually ate a meal with the missionaries, their anger grew into action. No Brahmin man should eat with anyone, Bengali or British, other than those in his caste. By breaking this rule, Kristna was saying that Christianity was true and the caste system and all the idol worship that went with it was not.

A mob attacked Kristna, beat him up and kidnapped his daughter. They forced her to marry a man who was not a Christian. After that, even though none of his friends would talk to him or do business with him, Kristna remained firm in his faith.

On December 28, 1800, William held a baptismal service. After the worship service in the newly built church, William led the congregation down to the river. There they met Colonel Bie, a number of curious Europeans, and a large group of Bengali people. William took the opportunity to preach a few words of explanation about baptism. He was careful to say that the water was just water, not sacred the way the Hindu religion said. And the act of baptism was to show that a Christian had put off all sins and put their faith in Christ. Then he led his oldest son, Felix, down into the water where he gently laid Felix down under the water and lifted him up again saying, "In the name of the Father, and the Son, and the Holy Ghost." After Felix, Kristna Pal entered the river and was baptized too.

Kristna's conversion was the turning point for the Serampore Mission. Others, who had either seen or heard about Kristna's public profession of faith, began to ask William and other missionaries, questions about God. Kristna began to preach to his fellow Bengalis. He built a preaching hut to hold up to forty people, where he urged the people to turn to Christ. First, his extended family became Christians, including his daughter and her husband, and then one of his close friends. Over the following year, more and more people turned their backs on their Hindu religion and became followers of Christ. Each one had to 'break their caste' by eating with other Christians, regardless of which caste any of them came from. After that, William joyfully baptized them in the river.

The opposition didn't stop though. Those who had professed faith knew they would have to endure anger and possibly physical violence from family and friends. But that only made their commitment to Christ even stronger. William had plodded on, expecting God would do great things, and now he was rejoicing to see so many coming to Jesus.

Plodding On
(1806-1812)

Not only did the Bengali people begin to respond to the gospel, but so did many of the Europeans who had come to India for work or a change of scene. Shortly after the mission was established in 1800, a thirty-nine-year-old Danish woman named Charlotte Rumohr arrived in Bengal. Charlotte was the daughter of Danish Count Chevalier de Rumohr. When she was fifteen, she woke to find the family home on fire. She was rescued but not without injuries. Even after her father had sent her to many doctors all over Europe, Charlotte was not able to walk and had difficulty speaking. But Charlotte was not idle. She loved to read and studied to learn to read French and Italian literature, along with Danish. Eventually her doctors recommended that Charlotte try living in India, thinking that the warm climate might help her disability. First, she moved to the south of India, to Tranquebar, a Danish colony. Then in November 1800, she moved to Serampore. The climate did make some difference. Charlotte found she could walk very short distances and speak more clearly, which encouraged her to want to learn another language, English. Colonel Bie suggested she should contact William Carey to teach her.

William gladly became Charlotte's tutor. He came to her home, which was not far from the Mission, once a week to be her tutor. He found Charlotte a quick learner and her studies moved along well. As her facility with English improved, they began to discuss various topics, including the Bible. Charlotte listened with interest as William shared the gospel with her. She even began to come to church to hear William and other missionaries preach. Their preaching convicted her of her sin, and eventually Charlotte was converted. In 1803, she asked William if she could be baptized, to which he readily agreed. Although her health did not fully recover, Charlotte wanted to help the mission work, so she offered the one thing she could, her wealth. And she began to learn Bengali with the hope that she could help out in the girls' schools. God was drawing people from various parts of the world to help in the Mission.

* * *

"God has done great things over these last six years," William said, as he leaned back in his chair. Both Joshua Marshman and William Ward heartily agreed. By 1806, the three were the only men left of the original group that began the Serampore Mission, and they became known as the Serampore Trio. Sadly, Mr. Fountain and Mr. Brunsdon had died within a year of arriving, and

Dr. Thomas too had passed away. Their wives had stayed on, helping with the mission work and in the schools. In spite of the loss of these men, the work had carried on.

"The number of conversions is wonderful," William Ward replied. "And the two mission stations we have been able to set up have helped to spread the gospel further."

"Yes, even into the city of Calcutta!" Joshua Marshman agreed. "God has really used your appointment as Professor of Sanskrit and Bengali to the Fort William College to allow us to preach in the city."

William had been surprised when the British East India Company asked him to teach the local languages to their incoming officials. Even though the Company still did not approve of the missionary work, they did recognize that they needed William's help with the languages. As a result, William came to Calcutta on a weekly basis to teach at the college and then to do some street preaching as well. Those who were converted, asked to set up their own mission station to reach others in the busy city. His salary from the college also helped support the other work of the Mission.

"One thing that does trouble me about the young men I'm teaching," William said, "They seem to think that they are superior to the Bengali people, as if India couldn't manage without the British East India Company. Although I'm only supposed to teach them the Bengali language, I'm trying to get them to see who the people really are. They aren't ignorant savages. They are intelligent people, who have different ways from us, which are not all bad."

Joshua agreed, "Those young men need to see that the work they will be doing will serve the Bengali people."

William nodded. "Yes, they need to think of themselves as public servants, not masters. I will do my best to make that part of my language instruction. Sometimes new attitudes quietly suggested rather than lectured on can make change easier."

* * *

Both Marshman and Ward had worked as hard as William did. Mr. and Mrs. Marshman had been very successful with their boarding schools as well as the free day school for the poor. The fees collected from the boarding schools now supported the free school. All of this meant that the Serampore Mission was not dependent on the Baptist Mission Society in England to keep sending them money. Marshman also assisted with the translations because of his ability to learn languages as quickly as William.

Mr. Ward was a first-class printer. Not only did he oversee the printing shop where William's translations of the Bible were printed, but he first had designed the fonts and types for languages very different from English. He even set up a papermaking shop to make sure that the Serampore Press had a steady supply of paper. So far, Ward had printed a complete Bengali New Testament, the Gospel of Matthew in Marathi, and two grammar books: one in Sanskrit and the other in Marathi.

The one area of sorrow for William was his wife, Dolly. He had hoped that being with other women in the mission would help her recover from her mental illness. But that did not happen. In fact, she got worse, becoming more and more violent and having to be locked in her room for her own safety and for the safety of others. Some suggested Dolly might be better in an asylum, but William couldn't bear the thought of her being cared for by people who didn't know and love her. Hannah Marshman, and the other women in the Mission, handled Dolly's care with great kindness.

In 1807, William had the joy of ordaining his oldest son, Felix. Twenty-one-year-old Felix was chosen to be sent as a missionary to Burma, and William was very proud of his son. He had a list of instructions for him, which included learning the Burmese language thoroughly, and not just enough to get by.

"By learning a people's language, you learn about the people themselves, what they believe and what they value," William told him. "And be sure to set up schools, so people can learn to read and write their own language, and especially read the Bible."

As a last request, he asked Felix to collect seeds for plants new to him and send them to him. William had plans to include them in his ever-growing garden of exotic plants and flowers.

In December that year, Dolly caught a fever that would not go away. As ever, William could hear her calling out in the next room while he worked on his translations in the evening. Then, one night, it was very quiet. Hannah Marshman knocked on his study door and came in.

"William, I think we need to call the doctor. Dolly hasn't woken up at all today, and I don't know what else I can do for her."

William immediately did as Hannah suggested and waited anxiously while the doctor was with Dolly in her room. When he came out, he shook his head.

"I'm sorry, Mr. Carey. Your wife is very poorly and is in a coma. There is not much anyone can do for her now."

William paid the doctor and then went to his study to pray. A week later, Dolly died. She was buried in the Serampore cemetery. Everyone was sad, but also relieved. Dolly was no longer suffering. She was at peace with her Savior in heaven.

* * *

While the missionary work carried on in 1808, William startled the entire mission staff with an announcement. He had asked Charlotte Rumohr to marry him.

"You can't marry so soon after Dolly's death!" Joshua Marshman exclaimed. "It's only been five months."

William tried to explain. "I know that, but for a long time Dolly was not able to be a companion to me because of her illness. Charlotte is a kind, Christian woman and as you know, very interested in helping the Mission. Since we have the same goal to serve Christ here in Bengal, why should we not marry?"

This answer did not entirely satisfy Joshua or the others, but William went ahead regardless. Charlotte and William, both forty-seven years old, were married in a small ceremony and she moved into William's apartment in the Mission House. In turn Charlotte donated her house and property to the Mission. Over time, the other missionaries accepted the marriage, especially because Charlotte cared so well for William and was willing to do whatever was needed at the Mission. She also took a great interest in William's sons, and they developed an affection for their stepmother.

* * *

The following year, the entire mission group rejoiced when William Ward brought the first copy of the entire Bengali Bible to show everyone. They each passed it around, opening it randomly and admiring the printed words.

"I also have the type set to print the complete New Testament in Sanskrit," Mr. Ward announced. "By the end of the year, we will have over a thousand copies of the Bible in these languages. Just think of all the people who will be able to read God's Word in their own language. Praise God!"

While William was very pleased with this big step forward, he knew there was still much to do. There were many other languages and dialects spoken by people all over Bengal. He and Joshua kept up their translation work each evening, in the hope of translating at least some part of the Bible into thirty languages or dialects. It would take a lifetime to accomplish it all, but they were happy to do the slow, painstaking work for the people of Bengal.

* * *

All continued to go well until March of 1812, and then disaster hit. William was in his lodgings in Calcutta, getting ready to teach at the Fort William College, when he heard an urgent knocking on his door. Joshua Marshman almost fell into the room when William opened the door. He was covered in soot and looked exhausted.

"Sit down," William urged him. "Tell me what has happened."

Joshua collapsed into the chair as tears ran down his dirty face. "It's all gone, the entire print shop, the printing press, all the translation work, everything … burned up."

William sat down heavily on his bed. "All of it?" he whispered.

Joshua nodded. "The fire started last evening and we thought we had it under control when someone opened a window. The air rushed in and caused the flames to reignite, and we could no longer stay in the building. By two this morning it had all burned down to the ground. I came to tell you as soon as I could."

Neither man spoke for a few minutes, thinking about all the work that had taken years to produce. Just gone in a few hours.

Then William said, "We need to pray. This is not a random act, but all part of the providence of God. He has promised that all things work for good to them who love God. Let's ask him to give us peace and direction."

Together, the two men knelt down and prayed, especially asking for the energy to keep on going with the work of the mission and not to give up.

Rebuilding
(1812-1827)

The next day, William called the dispirited mission staff together. "We will not give up God's work. We are going to find a new building, and start the printing shop again. Mr. Ward will be in charge of purchasing a new printing press. Mr. Marshman and I will begin the translation work again. We will replace everything that was destroyed and use it to God's glory."

William's speech inspired everyone and they started to help with whatever needed doing. Mr. Ward found a new printing press for sale and purchased it. A new building was purchased too, and just four months later, the Baptist Mission Press was in operation. William and Joshua Marshman spent long hours working on the translations, finding it easier this time because they remembered much of their work that had been lost in the fire. The Serampore Trio praised God for being able to eventually replace all the translation work.

* * *

In 1815 , William received a letter from England telling him that his good friend Andrew Fuller had died. He was the last of the group of men who had founded the Baptist Mission Society. William was sad to think that his steady supporter and fundraiser was now gone, and that he would no longer receive Andrew's encouraging letters. Unfortunately, Mr. Fuller's death also meant trouble in the Society. A younger group of men took over the responsibilities of running the mission in England and not all of them approved of the Serampore Trio's plans and methods. And that caused trouble in the Serampore Mission itself. Since 1813, when the British parliament issued an amendment to the East India Company's charter allowing missionaries to legally enter India, more missionaries had arrived wanting to help William. However, some did not always like William's way of doing things. Now that the leaders back home were also disagreeing with the Trio, discontent began to bubble up at the Saturday meetings of the mission staff. To make the matter even worse, William's nephew, Eustace Carey, was the spokesman for the group.

"Uncle, we know that a lot of money is coming in from the boarding schools, your college salary and other places. But we don't know where it all goes," Eustace said accusingly. "Is it going into your pocket? Or maybe you share it with Mr. Marshman and Mr. Ward?"

William could only stare in amazement. He was used to opposition from the Hindu people, but now his own nephew was turning against him. "NO!" William practically shouted when he found his voice. Then he took a deep breath and said in a quieter tone, "Any money I receive goes straight into the Mission's fund. I only keep back enough to meet the needs of my wife and sons. And Mr. Marshman and Mr. Ward do the same. We are not gathering any riches to ourselves, and I'm sorry you should say such a thing."

"That's what the Mission Society back in England think. And I do wonder, myself. You three men should not control everything that goes on in the Mission. Why not include some of us in your decisions about the money, on where it should be spent and on whom."

The meeting then erupted into everyone speaking and arguing at once. It broke William's heart to see it. "Gentlemen, please. We should not argue among ourselves. It is not right. It hurts the mission work."

But no one would listen. Eventually, the meeting broke up with Eustace leading the younger missionaries out of the Serampore Mission, planning to start their own mission in Calcutta.

William spent many sleepless nights reviewing all that had happened to cause Eustace and the other missionaries to leave Serampore. But, try as he might, he couldn't see what he could have done differently. He knew that the money was being used properly for the mission work. He could spend a lot of effort trying to convince the younger missionaries to return to Serampore, but he finally decided to leave the matter up to God.

Even though William was still hurt by his nephew's actions, he kept plodding on. He continued to set up schools because he knew the importance of education. By 1817, the mission had opened 103 schools throughout Bengal with over a total of 6,700 students. The growth of the schools had been slow at first. Parents felt uneasy sending their children to be educated by English men and women. Part of Hindu superstition was that educated young women would become widows shortly after they married, so they were kept at home to protect them. And others worried that their children would be kidnapped and taken away to England. But the missionaries persevered, encouraging parents to let their children come to the schools. Slowly, attitudes changed as those who did attend came home able to read and write, along with understanding arithmetic, geography, and science. More important than that, the students also learned about God's Word.

In 1818, the Serampore Trio decided there was a need to start a college, and they began to discuss plans for it.

"While we missionaries are doing the best we can to evangelize and disciple Christians, we can't do it all," Joshua Marshman began. "We need to be training up young native men to become ministers in their local churches."

"Yes," William Ward agreed. "And we must make it available to all men regardless of caste, color or even what country they come from."

William Carey added, "We should teach more than just theology, although that is the best of subjects. We need to teach all subjects, especially the sciences."

The other two laughed, knowing William's love of science, especially botany.

William smiled too and continued, "They need to know astronomy, so that they combat the Hindu notion that astrology controls people's lives. And, yes, botany too. After all, Psalm 145:10 says: 'All your works shall give thanks to you, O LORD.' Our students need to understand that the created world speaks about God. He is our creator and sustainer."

And so it was agreed. That year, the college opened with thirty-seven students. Each year the student body grew, so that soon they needed a bigger building. In 1822, a large two-story white building was completed. The decorative iron gates to the grounds and a wide porch with eight tall columns at the front of the building, gave it a grand look. The grounds were planted with trees and flowerbeds, making it a welcoming place for both students and teachers.

William never lost his love of plants and flowers. His own garden had grown to five acres of numerous plants and trees and he found much joy and relaxation working in it. He also became friends with Dr. William Roxburgh, the Superintendent of the Botanic Garden in Calcutta. Their shared interest led William to write an introduction to Dr. Roxburgh's book *Hortus Bengalensis, a catalog of the plants in the Botanic Garden*, which was published in 1814. After Dr. Roxburgh died, the British East India Company appointed another superintendent, but he had to return to Britain due to ill health. William did not want the work of the Garden to stop, so he founded the Agricultural and Horticultural Society of India in 1820, to encourage continued research and preservation of native plants and trees.

* * *

"I love our garden," Charlotte said from her chair that was set in the shade of a mahogany tree. "And I love watching you work in it."

William smiled and stood up, shaking the dirt off his hands, and brushing off his trousers. He sat down beside her and took her hand. "I'm glad you feel well enough to be out here. Do you need anything? Are you warm enough? Thirsty?"

Charlotte shook her head. "Don't fuss, William. I'm fine. I just wish I wasn't such a burden, having to be carried everywhere."

"You are not a burden," he assured her.

William was worried about his wife. In the thirteen years they had been married, she had never been strong, but now that she was sixty years old, she was becoming frail, and had lost the ability to walk again. However, her spirit was strong, and she insisted on joining in all the activities she could. William carried her down to the community dinners and out into the garden on the nice days. He arranged for her to be carried back and forth to church. But by the end of May 1821, Charlotte could no longer hold out against her increasing weakness. She died on May 30th.

William was full of grief. The companionship and love they had shared had been very special to him, and now he felt lost and lonely. His sons were grown and had families of their own. Most of them were serving as missionaries in various mission stations around India. He found it hard to concentrate alone in his rooms, being used to having Charlotte always nearby.

The following year, he met Grace Hughes, a middle-aged English widow, who had become interested in the mission's work. Her four children were grown and living on their own, so she filled her time with helping in the mission work. The more time William spent working with her, the more he thought she would make a good companion and wife. So, at the age of sixty-one, William married for a third time.

William's personal happiness was weakened later that year when first Kristna Pal died and then his oldest son, Felix. Felix had not done well as a missionary to Burma. He became more interested in politics than preaching the gospel. Then, his first wife died in childbirth and his second wife and children died in a shipwreck. Felix returned to Bengal full of grief and with no money. While he tried to help in the mission work, he eventually gave himself up to alcohol and drugs. His death in November 1822 was not a surprise to anyone.

The year 1823 brought more loss. The monsoon rains that year were like the one's William remembered in 1799 in Mudnabatti. The rain never seemed to let up over the summer months until once again the rivers overflowed their banks, flooding the mission school building and all but wiping out William's beloved garden. Once the waters receded, the mission staff got busy repairing or replacing the damaged parts of the schools, and William employed some helpers to try and restore his garden.

In the midst of all this activity, William Ward caught cholera and soon died of the disease. One of the Serampore Trio was now gone. However, Mr. Ward had trained his printing staff well and they were able to carry on with printing all the translations that William and Joshua Marshman continued to complete. In 1825, the press published William's Bengali/English dictionary, which was a great help to those learning the languages. In fact, William and Joshua, with the help of a team of Bengali scholars, had translated large portions of Scripture into thirty-four languages or dialects that were spoken in India. They also translated various grammar books and dictionaries in those languages. And Mr. Ward had made the publishing possible by designing the fonts and types for each language. God had used the talents of these men to accomplish the great task of translating the Bible.

The quarrels with the new group running the Baptist Mission in England had continued since

William's nephew had left the Serampore Mission. Eustace and even Jabez, William's younger son, had sent bad reports about Serampore and especially Joshua Marshman, who they claimed was imperious to the younger missionaries. William tried to bring peace, but no one would listen. Finally, Joshua and William decided to cut their ties with the English Baptist Mission and its counterpart the Calcutta Mission in 1827. William didn't want to spend his time fighting with fellow believers, but to get on with preaching the gospel and translation work. The only problem was, where was the money for the Serampore Mission going to come from?

The Final Years
(1828-1834)

William and Joshua struggled on for the next three years, eking out what few resources they had, to keep the Serampore Mission operating, as well as the nineteen mission stations that had been set up around Bengal. William was grieved that all this in-fighting had led to a separation from his son and nephew, as well as making the mission work itself more difficult. In 1830, both William and Joshua, now in their sixties, realized they could not continue the Serampore Mission on their own. They had run out of money and needed help. So, William wrote to England and offered to return to the Baptist Mission Society. They agreed to reunite with one condition. The Baptist Mission would now own all the property in Serampore and the other mission stations and all missionaries would be working for them. Joshua and William had a condition of their own: that they could stay and work in Serampore until they died. And so it was decided.

* * *

Throughout his time in Serampore, William had never given up his fight to end the terrible practice of suttee. Ever since he had witnessed the burning of the wife of a Brahmin man at the man's funeral, he did everything he could think of to get the practice banned. He spoke often to British officials, the governors who came and went, and the Bengali people themselves. But no one did anything about it. Then Lord William Bentinck was appointed Governor General of India. Lord Bentinck was a Christian, and he knew India well, having served in the British army in India for many years. Because he had a great deal of respect for the Bengali people, he wanted to make their lives better. William saw his chance to speak up.

"Thank you for being willing to see me, Lord Bentinck," William began as he was shown into the Governor General's office. "There is so much I would like to speak to you about."

Lord Bentinck smiled and gestured for William to sit down. "I've heard about you and the work your mission has been doing. You have done much to help the Bengali people, especially with your schools and all your translation work. So, how can I help you?"

"I have heard that you are planning some reforms for Bengal." The Governor-General nodded and waited for William to continue. "I'm sure you have heard of, or maybe even seen, the terrible practice of suttee. We need to stop it. Women are dying needlessly. And the children too. The unwanted ones are left out in the forest to die. And others are sacrificed to appease their idols. Please, please will you pass laws to stop this wickedness."

"Yes, I'm aware of all those wicked practices too. I've even seen them," he said with a shudder. "Things have to change. I have plans to reform the legal system, particularly to help those in the lower castes who live in poverty."

William interrupted Lord Bentinck at this point. "The level of usury is terrible, and leads to so much poverty. Could you include plans for savings banks too, so that people don't need to borrow money at such high interest rates?"

"That's an excellent idea," Lord Bentinck replied. "I'll add that to the list, but I think the suttees and cases of infanticide need to be addressed first. All people need to be protected, even children."

Lord Bentinck drew up a law in 1829 that made the practices illegal. He then asked William to translate the new law into as many languages as possible, so all people would know. William was overjoyed. At last, these women and children would be protected. He even missed church one Sunday morning to finish the translation work, thinking that God would see this as a good and necessary thing to do. The law caused upset because many Hindus saw this as interference in their religion. Nevertheless, the law was enforced wherever the practices were found.

In 1832, William finished his last translation project, a final revision of the Bengali New Testament. William had revised much of his work over the years, correcting the grammar or finding better words in Bengali to use. Translation work is much more than just replacing one English word with one in a different language. The context, or the meaning of a whole sentence or paragraph, must be communicated both clearly and accurately. William knew it was very important to organize the words well and choose the right phrases. He worked hard to make his translations sound as natural as possible to the people who spoke each language. Otherwise, people might find the translation difficult to read and understand, and then not want to read it. He also knew that his translations were not perfect, and he hoped that others would take up the work when he was gone.

* * *

"William? William! Are you well?" Grace asked her husband. When he didn't respond, she shook him gently by the shoulder. He was sitting in a chair on their veranda, looking out over his garden, or so she thought.

William heard his wife, but for some reason he couldn't speak or move. He wasn't sure what had happened to him. He had just been enjoying the early morning, watching the colorful birds that flew about the garden. Maybe he had fallen asleep?

A little later a doctor arrived and began to check William over carefully. William followed him with his eyes, but he still couldn't speak or move.

"Can you move your arm?" the doctor asked. "Or just your fingers?"

William tried and after a few attempts managed to wiggle his fingers. By the time the doctor finished his examination, William began to have feeling in parts of his body again, much to his relief.

"I think your husband has had a small stroke," the doctor said turning to Grace. "The best thing for him is rest. He may regain the use of the legs and speech with time. Meanwhile, please ask one of the young men to give me a hand carrying Mr. Carey inside.

Once in bed, Grace made William as comfortable as she could. She kissed him on the forehead and assured him that she would stay with him, and that the doctor would return the next day.

It was several days before William's speech came back and another few weeks before he was able to walk again. All the time he was recovering, he wrote many letters to friends and family in England as well as to his sons: William Jr., Jabez, and Jonathan. He thought they should know that his body was beginning to wear out.

William experienced several more small strokes over the last two years of his life. Grace nursed him through all of these episodes and each time he was able to recover and continue writing letters, do some preaching, and enjoy working in his garden. He also received many visitors. Some were new missionaries coming to join the Serampore Mission or going on to work with other missions. Some were government officials, and others who were interested in his botany work. Whoever arrived at his door, he never let them go without sharing the gospel with them, and encouraging new missionaries to plod on even when the work was difficult.

Finally, Grace sent messages to William's sons to come to him. William was weakening more and more after each stroke. The young men all arrived in time to see their father before he died on June 9, 1834. He was seventy-three years old. Before he died, he told his sons what he wanted written on his grave stone. William had always found the hymns written by Isaac Watts a great comfort, so he asked for one particular phrase from the hymn 'Lord, Help My Unbelief.'

A guilty, weak, and helpless worm,
On thy kind arms I fall.

William knew that what he had accomplished in Bengal was all by God's grace. Without God, he was guilty of sin and as weak and helpless as a worm. But he knew that Jesus was waiting for him as he died, ready to receive him with open arms, and like a child, William would fall into his Savior's arms.

Afterword

After William died in 1834, only Joshua Marshman was left of the Serampore Trio. He carried on the work of the mission for three more years before he died too. With the three founders of the mission now in heaven, much of the work was taken up by the Baptist Mission in Calcutta. Although the Serampore Mission did not exist anymore, there were still many missionaries living and preaching the good news of Jesus Christ. William Carey had led the way and inspired many to take up the work he and the Serampore Mission began.

God accomplished a great many things through William Carey because William was willing to serve God with his whole heart. He may have begun as a simple shoemaker with very little formal education, but by the time of his death William had become a translator, social reformer, botanist, pastor and much more. William knew that the gospel changed not only people's hearts, but their whole lives. His love for the Bengali people led him to become involved with the needs of the entire society.

William was not a perfect man. He was a sinner saved by God's grace, like all Christians. William made mistakes, and his biggest mistake was bringing his first wife, Dolly, to Bengal. Dolly was content being a mother and a pastor's wife in England. She didn't feel the same call to the mission field that her husband did, and she resisted going with him. She finally gave in after Dr. Thomas alternately coaxed her good naturedly and lectured her about supporting her husband. We don't know if Dolly would have developed a form of mental illness if the Carey family had stayed in England, but we do know that the difficult life in Bengal, the fear of the unknown, and the death of one of their sons contributed to her illness. There were very few good treatments for mental illness in the nineteenth century. The only real choices were asylums where people were treated like prisoners, or caring for the person at home. Even in the twenty-first century, doctors still don't know how to treat all types of mental illnesses. There are medications and therapies that work for some, but not for all patients.

William knew he had made a mistake bringing his wife to Bengal against her will. But he did do his best to make sure she was cared for. And he learned from this mistake. He advised the Baptist Mission Society to interview both the husbands and wives about going to the mission field. If the wives were not willing, then the Mission Society should not approve them. Other mission societies began to follow this advice too.

William also learned a personal lesson about marriage; about how important it is to marry someone who has the same interests. While all three of William's wives were Christians, they were all very different people. Dolly had had little formal education and was not interested in learning more, which meant she and William did not share many of the same interests. Charlotte, on the other hand, had received a very good education and was eager to keep learning languages, just like William. They shared many of the same interests. Grace was more like Dolly, with less education or interest in languages, but she was happy living in India, and she cared deeply for her husband.

God can and will use his imperfect children to do his work of spreading the gospel, whether at home or in a distant country. We don't have to be perfect, but we do have to be willing to serve God wherever we are living. God will accomplish great things for his glory, and he will do them through his people. Just look at how much William and the rest of the Serampore Mission accomplished.

Translation

Learning as many of the languages and dialects as possible in Bengal was one of William's main goals. In this way he could tell people the Good News of Jesus Christ. But he also knew that learning their languages helped him to understand the Bengali people, how they thought about life and what they believed. This gave him clues to the best words and phrases to use while he translated the Bible. William didn't stop at the Bible. He discovered some older writings in the old Sanskrit language that were useful for people to know, so he translated those too. Bengali scholars were very grateful for that, and they were more open to listening to William because he took their literature and language seriously.

Education

William believed very strongly that all people should receive education, both girls and boys, regardless of how much money their family had. Joshua and Hannah Marshman agreed with William, and they became the main teachers in the girls' and boys' schools that the Serampore Mission set up. They all agreed that all subjects should be taught, as well as sharing the gospel. This helped improve the Bengali way of life by giving them opportunities for jobs. The Serampore College that they set up, in 1818, is still operating in Calcutta today.

Natural Sciences

William thought it was important to study all of creation. The Hindu religion taught that their god was in all parts of the creation which made all parts sacred and able to be worshiped. William wanted them to understand that God created the world and all that is in it, which shows how great and wonderful God is.

He wanted them to worship God, not the things God created.

Botany

William was very interested in all aspects of science, but in particular he loved botany. He introduced the Linnaean system to gardening. The system is named after the man who invented it in the eighteenth century, Carl Linnaeus. He set up his system to put all organisms into classes naming them in an organized fashion.

Agriculture

While William traveled about preaching, he also did a systematic survey of agriculture in India. He noticed that large parts of the land could be used for cultivation of crops instead of letting them become overgrown. He wrote articles in journals urging agricultural reform so that the land could be used in a better way. As part of this idea, William also taught and wrote about cultivating and using timber wisely.

Astronomy

William taught and encouraged the study of astronomy to combat the wrong Hindu teaching of astrology. Astrology teaches that the movement of stars and planets affects people's lives. Instead, William wanted the people to understand that God created the stars and planets to help keep time and to be an added beauty to his creation.

Medicine

William and Dr. John Fleming wrote *A Catalogue of Indian Medicinal Plants and Drugs, with their Names in the Hindustani and Sanskrit Languages.* This was a great help to doctors. William also campaigned for more humane care for people with leprosy. People with leprosy were often badly mistreated, and William wanted that to stop.

Economy

William introduced the idea of a savings bank in India to stop the high levels of usury. Before there were banks in India, people who needed money would borrow from wealthy people. When it came time to repay that money, a high rate of interest was demanded. People often had to pay twice as much as they had borrowed, which could reduce them to poverty. A savings bank could help the people set aside some money for times when they might need it, and not pay high interest rates. Psalm 15 describes how a righteous person should live, listing all the things a righteous person should not do, including usury.

Libraries

William introduced the idea of a lending library to encourage more literacy. People could not always afford to buy books, but they could borrow them from a library.

Printing and Publishing

The Serampore Trio set up the largest printing press in India and used it to publish all the translation work they did. This included all the Bible translations as well as some Indian classic writing. They produced the first weekly magazine called *Friend of India*. It became very popular and included news from around India as well as international stories.

Social Reform

William advocated for many years to stop the Hindu practice of suttee to protect women whose husbands had died. He campaigned against child sacrifice and exposure, which were common Hindu practices. He also encouraged parents to let their girls be educated by setting up girls' schools.

Public Service

Through his teaching at the Fort William College, William helped to transform British attitudes in India. He encouraged new officials arriving from Britain to see their work as a public service to India. He wanted to stop the idea that the British were superior to the Indian people, and could therefore treat the Indian people as their servants.

* * *

See what God can do with a willing heart. He can take a person who doesn't appear to have much to offer and use him or her to accomplish much more than they or anyone else could imagine.

Glossary

Glossary

Astrology: the study of planets, stars, comets, etc. to interpret their influence on people and their lives. This is different from Astronomy that studies the same celestial bodies to understand the physical universe.

Asylum: an institution that housed people with mental illness. In the 18th and early 19th centuries the patients were often treated harshly.

Botany: the scientific study of plants and their importance.

British East India Company: A British company, chartered by the government in 1600 to carry on trade in Bengal, the eastern part of India. The company was dissolved in 1874.

Caste system: A society that is broken into classes which is determined by which family you are born into.

Cholera: an infectious disease caused by drinking infected water. In the nineteenth century it was usually fatal because there was no known cure at that time.

Covenant: an agreement between people. In biblical terms, covenants are agreements between God and his people.

Dialect: a sub group of a language which uses particular words or phrases only found in one region.

For example, English is spoken in large parts of the world, but often countries or regions may have words or phrases that are only used in that country, and may not be understood in other English-speaking places.

Dissenting Church: 17th and 18th century English Protestant churches that refused to be part of the Church of England.

Dysentery: an infectious disease that causes severe diarrhea and dehydration. There was no known cure in the nineteenth century.

Fonts and Types: nineteenth century printing presses required metal letters for each word. These metal letters were arranged in word order in a tray, covered with ink and then pressed onto paper. Each language required its own set of type and font.

Mantra: a word or sound that is repeated many times to help with concentration during meditation. In the Hindu religion, some mantras were considered better than others.

Ordination: a ceremony of dedicating a person to become a minister and authorized to perform the sacraments of baptism and the Lord's Supper.

Usury: the practice of lending money at an unreasonably high interest rate.

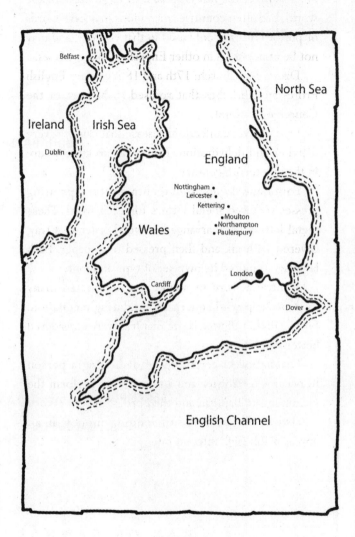

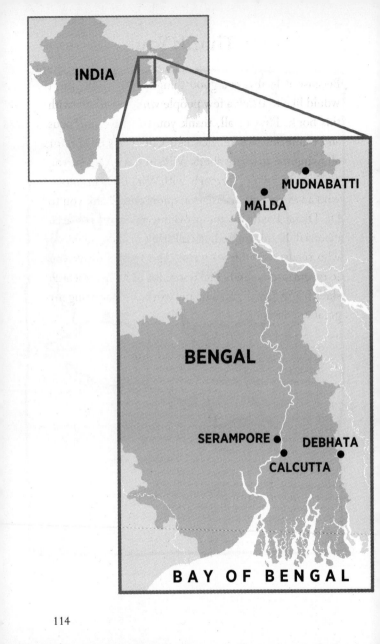

Thank You

Because it is always a good thing to say thank you, I would like to thank a few people who helped me with this book. First of all, thank you to Christian Focus and Catherine Mackenzie, their Children's Editor, for allowing me to write about William Carey. Thank you to Carmen Ewing, formerly with Wycliffe Translators, who answered my translation questions. Thank you to Dr. Diane Poythress for providing me with research material. Thank you to Donna Farley, my faithful friend who reads everything I write. And finally, thank you to my husband, Sandy Finlayson, for using his research skills on my behalf, reading my work, and for being my great encourager.

William Carey
Timeline

1756 Dorothy (known as Dolly) Plackett Carey born Piddington, Northamptonshire.

1761 William Carey born near Paulerspury, England.

1767 Carey family moves into Paulerspury, where William's father becomes headmaster.

1776 Declaration of Independence in America.

1777 William is apprenticed to a shoemaker Clarke Nichols of Piddington.

1778 Captain James Cook discovers Hawaii.

1779 February 10: William is converted at a Dissenters' prayer meeting in Hackleton.

      John Newton's *Amazing Grace* is published in *Olney Hymns*.

1781 June 10: William Carey marries Dolly Plackett.

1782 Daughter Ann is born.

1783 October 5: William is baptized by Rev. John Ryland in Northampton.

1784 Daughter Ann dies of fever.

      Benjamin Franklin invents bifocals.

1784-85

      William reads Captain James Cook's sea voyage accounts and is awakened to the spiritual need of those populations.

1785 Carey family moves to Moulton where William becomes a schoolmaster.

1786 Son Felix is born.

1787 William is ordained at Moulton Baptist Church. Dolly is baptized.

1788 Son William is born.

1789 Son Peter is born.

William accepts call to pastor Harvey Lane Baptist Church in Leicester.

1789 French Revolution begins.

1790 Daughter Lucy is born.

1792 October 2: Baptist Missionary Society is founded. Daughter Lucy dies.

1793 January 9: William appointed missionary to India.

April 4: Failed attempt to sail to Bengal.

Son Jabez is born in England.

June 13: William sets sail from Dover with his entire family and Dr. Thomas.

November 11: arrives in Calcutta.

1794 Carey family moves to Mudnabatti to manage an indigo factory.

Son Peter dies. Dolly's mental illness begins.

1795 William completes Bengali translation of Genesis–Exodus and Matthew–Mark.

London Missionary Society founded.

1796 January: son Jonathan born.

William baptizes first European convert.

1797 William completes Bengali New Testament translation, and Genesis to Numbers translation.

1799 William witnesses a suttee and begins a campaign to make it illegal.

October: more missionaries arrive from England.

1800 January 10: moves to Serampore and establishes a missionary community.

December 28: William baptizes first Bengali convert Krishna Pal and his son Felix.

1801 February 7: Bengali New Testament and Bengali grammar are published.

April: William is elected Professor of Sanskrit and Bengali languages at Fort William College in Calcutta.

1803 Serampore Mission becomes self-supporting.

1804 British and Foreign Bible Society is founded.

1805 Mission is established in Calcutta.

1807 British slave trade is abolished.

Felix Carey is ordained and goes to Burma.

December 8: Dolly Carey dies.

1808 Sanskrit New Testament is published.

May 9: William marries Charlotte Rumohr.

1809 June 24: Serampore Press publishes entire Bible in Bengali (5 volumes).

1812 March 11: fire destroys the printing presses and all translation manuscripts.

June 24: Napoleon invades Russia.

1813 July 3: British East India Company charter is renewed by British parliament with a new clause allowing missionaries free access to India.

1814 William writes an introduction to William Rozburgh's *Hortus Bengaliensis*.

William ordains his son Jabez, who goes to the Moluccan Island, Indonesia.

1815 Punjabi New Testament and the Bengali dictionary are completed.

1818 Sanskrit Old Testament is published.

July: Serampore Trio founds Serampore College.

1820 September 14: William founds the Agricultural and Horticultural Society.

Marathi Old Testament is published.

1821 May 5: Napoleon Bonaparte dies.

May 30: Charlotte Carey dies.

1822 July 22: William marries Grace Hughes.

1825 Dictionary of Bengali and English is completed.

1827 March 17: Serampore Mission withdraws from Baptist Missionary Society.

1829 Law passed that makes suttee illegal in India.

1834 June 9: William Carey dies in Serampore, India.

1835 June 27: Grace Carey dies.

1837 June 20: Queen Victoria begins her reign.

Serampore Mission closes.

Selected Bibliography

These are some of the books I found helpful in writing this biography.

Beck, James R. *Dorothy Carey: the tragic and untold story of Mrs. William Carey*. Grand Rapids, MI: Baker Book House, 1996.

Carey, William. *The Journal and Selected Letters of William Carey*. Edited by Terry G. Carter. Macon, GA: Smyth & Helwys, 2000.

George, Timothy. *Faithful Witness: The Life and Mission of William Carey*. n.p.: Christian History Institute, 1998.

Haykin, Michael A.G. *The Missionary Fellowship of William Carey*. Sanford, FL: Reformation Trust, 2018.

Mangalwadi, Vishal & Ruth. *The Legacy of William Carey: a Model for the Transformation of a Culture*. Wheaton, IL: Crossway Books, 1999.

Pease, Paul. *William Carey: the Missionary to India Who Attempted Great Things for God*. Travel With series. Leominster: Day One, 2005.

Thinking Further Topics

1. Storm at Sea

William had never thought he would be a missionary in India, but he was willing to go wherever God called him to go to share the Good News of Jesus Christ. We ought to have the same attitude. We may not be sent to a different country, but we do know that many of the people we meet do not know about the Gospel. Are you ready to share the Good News with your friends? It can seem difficult because we worry about being laughed at. However, God will give us the courage if we ask him. (See Joshua 1:9)

2. Shoemaking

William was disappointed when he couldn't become a gardener like his uncle. Instead, his father sent him to learn about shoemaking. Even though William wasn't really interested in becoming a shoemaker, he was obedient. Sometimes our parents ask us to do things we'd rather not do, but God tells us in his Word that we should obey our parents because it is the right thing to do. In Ephesians 6:1-3, the Apostle Paul tells us that this command comes with a promise, that our lives will go well and we will have a long life.

3. Life Changes

God gives each of us gifts. He gave William the gift of learning languages easily. When William became a

Christian, he used the languages of Greek and Hebrew to help him learn and understand the Bible so he could preach to a small congregation. We need to use our gifts and talents to serve God too. The Apostle Paul writes about using our gifts for others in the church in 1 Corinthians 11:12-26. He compares our gifts to parts of the body, showing how each person contributes to the working of the church by using their gifts.

4. Preaching the Word

Have you ever heard people making excuses for not sharing the Gospel? William did, and he did his best to persuade his fellow ministers about the importance of following Jesus' command in Matthew 28:18-20. We too are to follow that command and tell our friends, and even our families if they are not Christians, about God's love.

5. Off to Bengal

Sometimes friends can disappoint us. Dr. Thomas should have been more open with William and the Baptist Mission Society about his debts. The result was that William couldn't provide for his family when they first arrived in Bengal. However, even when people let us down, God never does. Proverbs 18:24 tell of a friend who sticks closer than a brother, and that is the Lord Jesus Christ.

6. Mudnabatti

Unexpected things happen. William knew Dolly wasn't happy, but he never expected that she would become ill in her mind. He did the best he could, getting her medical help and praying. Praying is the very best thing we can do when something difficult or upsetting happens. In Hebrews 4:16 we are told that we can come to God and he will give us grace and mercy to help in our time of need.

7. Monsoon!

Do you ever feel discouraged when you work hard at something and it doesn't turn out the way you wanted? William often felt that way. He worked hard at his job and at telling people the Good News of Jesus Christ. And all that happened was his job was washed away in the flood and none of the villagers became Christians. But he didn't give up. He knew the Lord would give him strength to carry on. (See Isaiah 40:31)

8. Serampore

Kristna Pal, the first Bengali convert, had a very difficult time when he was first converted. He was beaten up and none of the Bengali people would do business with him. But he stood firm in his faith. We can be tempted to deny being a Christian rather than being left out of a group or activity. Sometimes it doesn't seem fair that we have to suffer in any way for being a Christian. But that is the time we should remember just how much Jesus suffered for us. He was beaten, laughed at, and finally nailed to a cross to take our punishment.

9. Plodding On

Translation work is not every exciting. William and Joshua Marshman put in long hours translating parts of the Bible into many different languages, and William Ward spent just as long laying out and printing all those translations. Sometimes the tasks we are called to do seem to take such a long time that we wonder if we will ever finish. In Galatians 6:9 the Apostle Paul encouraged the Galatian Christians to "not grow weary of doing good, for in due season we will reap, if we do not give up." William knew the translation work was part of his doing good, and so he did not give up.

10. Rebuilding

William had a hard time of it with opposition from the younger missionaries, including his nephew and youngest son. Sadly, Christians often disagree with each other when they should be working together to serve God. Most times it happens out of jealousy, pride, or bad temper, all sinful attitudes. In Colossians 3:12-14 we are told to be kind, patient and humble, forgiving each other just as God has forgiven us.

11. The Final Years

The practice of suttee was a terrible thing. William cared deeply about the women who were killed this way, and for the babies who were killed or abandoned because of the Hindu religion. It took courage to continue speaking out about it, but eventually, after thirty-two years, the authorities listened and passed laws to abolish the practices. If William had gotten tired of waiting for change, the laws may never have been made. God rewards perseverance for good. (See 2 Chronicles 15:7)

12. Afterword

God used William Carey to accomplish a great deal in Bengali society during his lifetime. William was willing to serve God with his whole heart, just as every Christian should. Serving God means putting aside our wants and desires to do what God has commanded us to do. And we will be rewarded for being good and faithful servants. Matthew 25:21

Thomas Clarkson

The Giant With One Idea

Emily J. Maurits

- Biography for 9–14s
- British abolitionist
- Part of the successful Trail Blazers series

Thomas Clarkson was the son of a clergyman who lived in a time when it was legal to buy and sell slaves. He believed this was wrong, and campaigned to make sure this changed. He was instrumental in making sure that no human being could be bought or sold in the British Empire.

ISBN: 978-1-5271-0677-2

OTHER BOOKS IN THE
TRAIL BLAZERS SERIES

CHRISTIAN FOCUS PUBLICATIONS

Christian Focus | Christian Heritage | CF4K | Mentor

Christian Focus Publications publishes books for adults and children under its four main imprints: Christian Focus, CF4K, Mentor and Christian Heritage. Our books reflect our conviction that God's Word is reliable and Jesus is the way to know him, and live for ever with him.

Our children's publication list covers pre-school to early teens. We also publish personal and family devotional titles, biographies and inspirational stories that children will love.

From pre-school board books to teenage apologetics, we have it covered!

Find us at our web page:
www.christianfocus.com

CF4·K
Because you're never
too young to know Jesus